AMERICAN MODERNISM
(1910–1945)

Jerry Phillips, Ph.D.
General Editor to First Edition

Department of English
University of Connecticut, Storrs

Michael Anesko, Ph.D.
Adviser and Contributor

Director, Honors Program in English
Pennsylvania State University

Roger Lathbury, Ph.D.
Patricia Linehan
Principal Authors

■ ■ ■ ■ ■

CHELSEA HOUSE
PUBLISHERS
An imprint of Infobase Publishing

American Modernism (1910–1945)

Copyright © 2010, 2006 by DWJ BOOKS LLC

DEVELOPED, DESIGNED, AND PRODUCED FOR CHELSEA HOUSE BY DWJ BOOKS LLC

Dedication

To Camille

Chelsea House
An imprint of Infobase Publishing
132 West 31st Street
New York NY 10001

Library of Congress Cataloging-in-Publication Data

Lathbury, Roger.
 American modernism (1910–1945) / Jerry Phillips, general editor; Michael Anesko, adviser
 and contributor; Roger Lathbury, Patricia Linehan, principal authors.—2nd ed.
  p. cm. — (Backgrounds to American literature)
 Includes bibliographical references and index.

ISBN 978-1-60413-488-9 (hardcover: alk. paper)

 1. American literature—20th century—History and criticism. 2. Modernism (Literature)—United States.
I. Phillips, Jerry (Jerry R.) II. Anesko, Michael. III. Linehan, Patricia, 1950- IV. Title. V. Series.
PS228.M63L38 2010
810.9'112—dc22   2009029632

Chelsea House books are available at special discounts when purchased in bulk quantities for businesses, associations, institutions, or sales promotions. Please call our Special Sales Department in New York at (212) 967-8800 or (800) 322-8755.

You can find Chelsea House on the World Wide Web at http://www.chelseahouse.com

Text design by DWJ BOOKS LLC
Cover printed by Bang Printing, Brainerd, MN
Book printed and bound by Bang Printing, Brainerd, MN
Date printed: April 2010
Printed in the United States of America

Acknowledgments
pp. 9, 23, 37, 49, 65, 77, 83: Library of Congress, Prints and Photographs Division
pp. 15, 25, 57: Courtesy Roger Lathbury
p. 87: NOAA George E. Marsh Album
p. 91, 101: The Granger Collection, New York

10 9 8 7 6 5 4 3 2 1

This book is printed on acid-free paper.

All links and Web addresses were checked and verified to be correct at the time of publication. Because of the dynamic nature of the Web, some addresses and links may have changed since publication and may no longer be valid.

Contents

Preface

■ ■ ■ ■ ■ ■ ■ ■ ■ ■ ■ ■ ■ ■ ■ ■ ■ ■ ■

The five volumes of *Backgrounds to American Literature* explore 500 years of American literature by looking at the times during which the literature developed. Through a period's historical antecedents and characteristics—political, cultural, religious, economic, and social—each chapter covers a specific period, theme, or genre.

In addition to the original six chapters, this second edition of *American Modernism* includes a seventh chapter focusing on the widespread cultural effects of America's GREAT DEPRESSION. Readers will find a useful timeline of drama and theatrical history, poetry and prose, and history; a glossary of terms (also identified by SMALL CAPITAL LETTERS throughout the text); a biographical glossary; suggestions for further reading; and an index. By helping readers explore literature in the context of human history, the editors hope to encourage readers to further explore the literary world.

1. American Modernism

Organized to commemorate the 400th anniversary of Columbus's discovery of the New World, the World's Columbian Exposition in Chicago in 1893 gave physical form to the American Dream. What was built at Chicago was a monument not only to Columbus but also to a society increasingly dominated by the power of corporations and other large-scale organizations that were overtaking traditional confidence in individuals' abilities to shape their own destinies.

In its earlier phases, capitalist economic development acquired a kind of "heroic" dimension: the self-made person became the cornerstone of American business mythology. And the dream of success was inevitably linked to middle-class ideals of thrift, the Protestant work ethic, and self-reliant perseverance. After the Civil War, however, the rise of large-scale organizations made the individual's role much more ambiguous.

It has often been said that modern American literature got off to a timely start in 1900 with the publication of Dreiser's first novel, *Sister Carrie*. Derided by genteel critics, *Sister Carrie* is a fable of success but without affirming the conventional moral formula that virtue will be rewarded and vice will be punished. Dreiser refuses to make moral judgments of his characters, and

■ ■ ■ ■ THE FERRIS WHEEL ■ ■ ■ ■

Jutting out perpendicularly from Daniel H. Burnham's majestic "Court of Honor" at the Columbian Exposition of 1893 ran the Midway Plaisance, a carnival of exotic and eclectic tastes. As the official handbook of the fair described it, the Midway was "a most unusual collection of almost every type of architecture known to man—oriental villages, Chinese bazaars, tropical settlements, ice railways, the ponderous Ferris wheel, and reproductions of ancient cities." At the very center of this strange amalgam stood the enormous amusement ride—the Ferris wheel.

From the point of view of design, Gustav Eiffel's Tower and Ferris's wheel have much in common: Both, essentially, are collections of steel beams and rivets. Likewise, both take the fundamental structural principle of another nineteenth-century invention (the steel-truss bridge) and thrust it vertically into the air, symbolically linking earth and sky. The Ferris wheel, however, Americanized the static vertical "bridge" of Eiffel by shaping it into a circle and setting it in motion, endlessly revolving, spinning on an axle.

they themselves seem incapable of recognizing their actions in terms of good or evil.

Admittedly, the principal American modernists—Gertrude Stein, Ezra Pound, T. S. Eliot, William Faulkner—would have claimed a different genealogy, tracing their descent from Henry James, not Dreiser. It was James, after all, who seemed to make living in Europe enviable for artists.

Modernism in literature was matched by modernism in the visual arts. In 1913, the ARMORY SHOW, a great exhibition of modern art on New York's Lexington Avenue, opened. This event brought works by Picasso, Kandinsky, Matisse, and Duchamp to an American audience for the first time, challenging conventional representation.

Whatever the instrument—poem, novel, canvas, play—the music to be heard was new. That, after all, was Pound's fundamental imperative: "Make it new." Rejecting their immediate cultural inheritance as barren and unworkable, the modernists sought to find what Van Wyck Brooks memorably called a "usable past." Pound, for example, eagerly translated poetry from Japanese, Chinese, and Provençal, influences that leave their traces throughout his work. T. S. Eliot's most famous poem, *The Waste Land* (1922), recognizes no boundaries of time or place. Its deliberately

■ ■ ■ ■ THE RISE OF BIG BUSINESS ■ ■ ■ ■

It remains one of the central paradoxes of modern history that while Americans have always been suspicious of concentrated power—a fear that lies behind the American Revolution itself and founding documents such as the federal Constitution—the United States also has given birth to the modern business corporation. The first nineteenth-century enterprises to prefigure the bureaucratic complexity of modern companies were the railroads. Because of their enormous appetites for capital, these ventures quickly became dependent on public initiatives (such as federal land grants) and Wall Street bankers to underwrite their investments in rights-of-way, rails, locomotives, and rolling stock.

At the end of the nineteenth century, other manufacturing enterprises (notably steel, meatpacking, and oil refining) recognized the tremendous competitive advantage of vertical integration—that is, extending corporate control to every aspect of production and distribution. Thus, Andrew Carnegie not only manufactured steel but he also bought up mines where all the elements for steel production came from (iron ore, coal, limestone) as well as railroad and steamship lines that carried those raw materials to Pittsburgh. When Carnegie combined his holdings with that of seven other metalworks to form U.S. Steel in 1901 (the nation's first billion-dollar corporation), the company controlled two-thirds of the country's steel market.

disjointed lines crisscross continents and centuries; the range of its allusions—literary, philosophical, theological—has captivated (and bewildered) critics and readers since the day it appeared

"These fragments I have shored against my ruins" (line 431 from *The Waste Land)* is a metaphor for modernist form. All the modernist artistic categories (literature, painting, sculpture, dance, musical composition) seem deliberately chaotic. Not surprisingly, first reactions to works of modernist art can be disorienting because it is often difficult to know even where they begin. When reading a poem, starting at the first line would seem to be obvious—but so many modernist first lines are completely (and deliberately) arbitrary that the reader (or viewer, or listener, as the case may be) might be inclined to think of the work as fundamentally inaccessible.

The Politics and Culture of Modernism

For many who experienced it, nothing could have been less genuine than America's involvement in World War I. In 1916, President

Woodrow Wilson was elected to a second term largely on the strength of a campaign slogan: "He kept us out of war." Shortly thereafter, he got us into a war that would usher in the modern era with a vengeance.

Unlike previous armed conflicts, where soldiers squared off on the battlefield and obeyed time-honored rules of engagement, World War I demonstrated the horrific potential of new technologies of destruction, the MECHANIZATION that made killing far less personal. World War I was the first in which airplanes, including the German ZEPPELINS, were used both for reconnaissance and attack. The Zeppelins were easily shot down, but the men inside the Zeppelin and the men on the ground did not see each other. Whether the soldiers were German or French, Italian or English, or American, machines and chemicals did the work of killing. Men died, but machines did the work.

World War I, then, was a brutal assault on the orderly civilization of the nineteenth century. In a quieter way, however, intellectual currents had been working to undermine "the sea of Faith" that the British poet Matthew Arnold saw as circling and nourishing "the earth's shore." In England, Charles Darwin (1809–1882) had published *The Origin of the Species* in 1859, a work that for many displaced traditional ideas of God as the creator of the universe. Also, in Vienna, Austria, in 1900, Sigmund Freud (1856–1939) rocked the world with his ideas about infant sexuality and his theories of personality, ideas that collectively came to be referred to as FREUDIAN.

The Interpretation of Dreams, as well as Freud's other studies of the workings of the human mind, suggested that men and women were ruled by dark forces of which they were unaware. Freud's studies opened a new window on the human mind just as Albert Einstein's (1879–1955) theories of relativity—also

■ ■ THE ARMORY SHOW ■ ■

The history of twentieth-century American art properly begins in 1913 with the International Exhibition of Modern Art held at the 69th Street Regiment Armory in New York City. Organized by artists who were eager to displace accepted modes of representation and anxious to make Americans aware of startling new developments arising in Europe, this colossal exhibition (1,300 paintings and pieces of sculpture) had the effect of a guillotine, severing a new generation from the moribund ideals of the past. The Armory Show provides a textbook example of what historians call a watershed event—a decisive turning point in cultural development. Though academic critics were disdainful in the extreme, and newspaper cartoonists could not resist the urge to satirize the "highbrow" nature of some of the works on display, the Exhibition was a popular success and, more importantly, a triumph of propaganda on behalf of modernism.

in circulation at the time—did on the physical world. Both thinkers seemed to say that humans were not in control of their own lives. At first Freud's ideas were met with skepticism, but acceptance of them grew until they pervaded the culture. In the late twentieth century, however, some experts began to question Freud's basic concepts.

Five Modernist Poets

T. S. Eliot (1888–1965)

Freud's influence on the climate of modern poetry can be seen in T. S. Eliot's "The Love Song of J. Alfred Prufrock" (1917). From the opening lines of "Prufrock," readers are in a different world from that of earlier poetry. Almost all original poetry seems obscure when first encountered, but some of the confusions in "Prufrock" are intentional.

> Let us go then, you and I,
> When the evening is spread out
>   against the sky,
> Like a patient etherized upon a
>   table . . .

> ■ ■ MEANINGLESS WORDS— ■ ■
> MEANINGLESS VIOLENCE
>
> In *A Farewell to Arms* (1929), his great novel about World War I, Ernest Hemingway's hero, Frederic Henry, suffers a terrible leg wound when his ambulance company on the Italian front is shelled. After a long recuperation, he comes to see not only that war is futile but also the way in which language has been manipulated to provoke and justify the senseless killing that surrounds him. At a crucial turning point in the novel, Henry reflects to himself, "Abstract words such as glory, honor, courage, or hallow were obscene beside the concrete names of villages, the numbers of roads, the names of rivers, the numbers of regiments and dates." No one was more adept at using "abstract words" than President Woodrow Wilson, whose administration pioneered the use of mass-media propaganda to overcome the country's traditionally isolationist stance toward Europe. In Wilson's view, America had a moral destiny "to make the world safe for democracy."

The poem never clarifies who "you and I" are; they may be Prufrock and the reader, or they may be Prufrock and a friend, real or imaginary. The first metaphor is unsettling in its understated strangeness. How can "evening" be compared to an "etherized patient"? The automatic association of these two images in Eliot's poem—like the free associations of one of Freud's patients during a therapy session—suggests a person entirely separated from his or her surroundings. Together with the succeeding stanzas, which project disassociated scenes of a future encounter with a person the poem names as "one," the poem seems hallucinatory, only half clear. This effect is paradoxically augmented

Wilson addressing Congress
President Woodrow Wilson (1912–1920) hoped World War I would be the war
to end all wars and to make the world safe for democracy. Here he is shown
addressing a 1916 joint session of Congress with his lofty plan. The League
of Nations, a forerunner of the United Nations, was one result of World War I,
but it did not succeed, as Wilson hoped it would, in preventing another war.

■ ■ ■ ■ FREUDIAN SYMBOLISM IN LITERATURE ■ ■ ■ ■
Sigmund Freud's discovery of the unconscious had a tremendous impact on
literary modernism. His hypotheses about sexual development and repres-
sion inspired radical possibilities for artists intent on exploring human mo-
tives and psychology.

Twentieth-century drama enthusiastically embraced Freudian themes, not
least because through them playwrights could escape from the hackneyed
traditions of melodrama that had virtually monopolized the American stage.
Because, at least in theory, Freud's concepts transcended the limits of historical time and space, they empowered a dramatist such as Eugene O'Neill
to envision his works not only as period pieces but also as occasions for
exploring the eternal tragedy of the human condition. In *Desire Under the
Elms* (1924), for example, O'Neill's opening stage directions fix a specific
historical setting, but they also suggest the power of psychological symbols
to go beyond the limits of realistic details. Note the symbolic power with
which he invests the elm trees:

> *The action of the entire play takes place in, and immediately outside of, the
> Cabot farmhouse in New England, in the year 1850. . . . Two enormous elms
> are on each side of the house. They bend their trailing branches down over the
> roof. They appear to protect and at the same time subdue. There is a sinister
> maternity in their aspect, a crushing, jealous absorption. . . . They brood op-
> pressively over the house. They are like exhausted women resting their sagging
> breasts and hands and hair on its roof, and when it rains, their tears trickle
> down monotonously and rot on the shingles.*

by the wit of the lines, many of which have entered the common
language:

> In the room the women come and go
> Talking of Michelangelo.
> . . . .
> I have measured out my life with coffee spoons.
> . . . .
> I grow old . . . I grow old . . .
> I shall wear the bottoms of my trousers rolled.

The musicality and suppleness of Eliot's rhythms, the intrigu-
ing, incompletely revealed dramatic situation, and the profusion

of details ("tea and cakes and ices") bring readers inexorably into participating in Prufrock's dilemma; the reader, too, feels alienated, puzzled, worried, incomplete.

Eliot's ability to project and intensify this sense of alienation reached its high point in *The Waste Land* (1922). Its five sections are a carefully orchestrated series of vignettes that point up the sterility—physical, emotional, and spiritual—of Western civilization. Although the poem is centered in London—where Eliot relocated in 1914—that city is incidental. It becomes a metaphor for other locales, until the poem embraces the entire world: London, Munich, Jerusalem, Athens, Alexandria, and Vienna are all named. The short scenes refer to classical, medieval, and modern times, equating them at will, alluding to previous literature from all periods, making the atmosphere of post—World War I despair seem to be a symptom of a larger, ineradicable uneasiness.

This 434-line poem, notorious for its difficulty when it was first published, became, for 50 years after its appearance, the dominant cultural artifact of the twentieth century. It is the purest example of a modernist poem: uncompromising in its aims, committed to effects of collage, making ALLUSION to other artistic products. The poem makes obscure and scholarly references that many readers did not understand. It seemed a total break with the nineteenth century—in other words, it was utterly and completely modern.

Out of a defeat as total as that portrayed in *The Waste Land,* what kind of life can be built? For Eliot, the answer was a return to religion. The process was gradual, and, as he retreated from the themes of *The Waste Land* and found Christian faith—Eliot joined the Anglican Church in 1930—his poetry changed as well. In place of the sharp epithet and collage, Eliot's poems, after *The Hollow Men* (1925), became more connected, at times serene; his modernism gives way to LYRICISM. The most renowned example of Eliot's lyricism is found in *Four Quartets* (1942). More abstract and less tense than the earlier work, these poems return to a conscious effort to affirm values, which they embody in carefully orchestrated subtlety.

Ezra Pound (1885–1972)

Like Eliot, Ezra Pound was a transplanted American. Born in Idaho, educated in Pennsylvania, Pound fled to Europe where he made modernism into a career. Pound is most often associated with IMAGISM, a poetic credo that he promulgated. Pound insisted that a genuine poem would focus on the "direct treatment of the

'thing' whether subjective or objective"; it would "use absolutely
no word that does not contribute to the presentation"; and it
would be composed "in the sequence of the musical phrase,
not in the sequence of a metronome." These principles are il-
lustrated by Pound's two-line poem of 1916 "In a Station of
the Metro."

> The apparition of these faces in the crowd;
> Petals on a wet, black bough.

The poem presents two images, directly, side by side. No verb
is needed for the presentation; therefore, no verb occurs. The
rhythm of the first line is mostly but not mechanically IAMBIC (the
APparItion of these FAces in the CROWD). Line two hammers its
point home with the three accented words at the close (PETals on
a WET, BLACK BOUGH).

Pound eventually broke from the confines of imagism. *Hugh
Selwyn Mauberly* (1920) makes a case against the intellectual nar-
rowness and lack of appreciation of beauty of the modern world by
using rather strict rhyme and rhythm—perhaps a reaction to the
tendencies toward formlessness of some imagists—and by the
wideness of its literary tastes. Mauberly—the poem's subject—is,
like Pound, a poet, but Mauberly has written only a single imagistic
poem, in the tradition of the late nineteenth century. In an impres-
sive array of meters and tones, with quotations in Greek and with
echoes of well-known poets of the past, such as Pindar, Horace,
Ronsard, Edmund Waller, and Theophile Gautier, Pound castigates
not only the aesthetic taste of his age but also the shallow tawdri-
ness of contemporary life.

A monument of modernism, *The Cantos* (1921), published bit by bit, in booklets, is a fluid mixture of all branches
of knowledge, judged through the understanding of the ancient Chinese philosopher Confucius. Throughout, Egyptian
hieroglyphics and Chinese IDEOGRAPHS mingle with social
theories.

The Cantos is probably the densest, most allusive poem in
English (or mostly in English), but individual cantos often rise to the
beauty and grandeur of which Pound was capable.

> What thou lovest well remains, the rest is dross
> What thou lov'st well shall not be reft from thee
> What thou lov'st well is thy true heritage

At their best, Pound's lines stir by the force of their argument and educate by challenging readers to see and hear afresh and so renew experience.

Gertrude Stein (1874–1946)

The writings of a third expatriate American are even more radical in their distance from conventional prose and poetry. It is not clear how to characterize the writings of Gertrude Stein. Stein's first book, *Three Lives* (1909), is less a narrative or story than a series of stylistic experiments. The reader becomes less involved with the characters than with the words on the page. The language of the story has less to do with referring to something or someone than with creating a pattern of sound or even sight.

Once established, the variations on that pattern create different emphases, effects, and layers of awareness in the reader who variously is absorbed in what is being said and detached from it by an awareness of its manner. Stein came by such design after moving to Paris, where she lived among experimental visual artists. With her lifetime companion Alice B. Toklas, Stein established a SALON. Long before they became well known, visual artists, such as Pablo Picasso, Marcel Duchamp, and Henri Matisse, and writers, including French poet Guillaume Apollinaire, and, after World War I, American expatriates, such as Sherwood Anderson, William Carlos Williams, T. S. Eliot, and Ernest Hemingway, visited her in her apartment at 27 rue de Fleurus.

Her own writing became progressively more experimental. *Tender Buttons* (1914) represents an intermediate step toward pure language. The book is a list, a collection of descriptions that sometimes connect to the object announced and sometimes do not.

> **Rhubarb.**
> Rhubarb is not susan not susan not seat in bunch toys not wild and laughable not in little places not in neglect and vegetable not in foal coal age not please.

It is easy to see such experiments as frivolous, or even fraudulent. Some have said that Gertrude Stein wrote in an eccentric way in order to acquire a reputation as a great artist and to feed her own ego. Stein's apparently arbitrary use of words invites misunderstanding. What is the connection of sound to sense?

Stein wrote other, more conventional books, including a bestseller, *The Autobiography of Alice B. Toklas,* in which traces of her distinctive, repetitive style show through. Her fame, however, comes from the experiments with words. Readers of her work saw that some of it consisted of APHORISMS. One of the most famous aphorisms is "rose is a rose is a rose," which suggests that beyond saying rose equals rose one can say nothing more—possibly a Platonic statement about perfection embodied in "Rose," whoever or whatever Rose may be.

E. E. Cummings (1894–1962)

Like Stein, E. E. Cummings first came to prominence when readers were stunned by his disregard for conventional language and syntax and by unconventional line breaks and "strangeness."

> ta
> ppin
> g
> toe

Like Stein, he ignored conventional punctuation. "If writing should go on what had colons and semi-colons to do with it?" Stein had asked. Cummings's poems cross the border between verbal and pictorial art. In one of his imagist experimentations, the words "1 leaf falling" are arranged vertically on the page like the leaf itself. None of his poems is titled: The reader must confront the poem itself.

Against his visual playfulness and experimentation, Cummings shows exuberant lyricism and satirical bite. Many of his famous poems—such as "all in green went my love riding" or "anyone lived in a pretty how town"—could be reset conventionally and readers would find them moving lyrical poems. However, the lowercase letters and lack of punctuation add immediacy; the "direct treatment of the 'thing,'" in Pound's words, underpins a fundamental innocence. This is a man impatient with pretension, apparently opposed to form, and not drawn to intellect or philosophy, religion or complex theory.

Marianne Moore (1887–1972)

Also living in England, but very much an outsider, was the American Marianne Moore. If Eliot, Pound, Stein, and Cummings were experimenting with language and convention, Moore's experiments were more directly formal. Most English poetry is written in accentual meter; the beats of the line follow a pattern, not, as Pound pointed

A gathering of modernists
From left to right are James Joyce, author of *Ulysses*; Ezra Pound, American poet;
Ford Maddox Ford, British novelist; and John Quinn, American patron of Joyce
and others. The picture was taken in Paris in the studio of Constantin Brancusi,
the sculptor, in 1924.

out, like a metronome, but essentially regular.

/ ˘   /   ˘   /   ˘   /
April   is   the   cruellest month

Marianne Moore's poetry rejects accentual meter in favor of
SYLLABICS. Her stanza patterns are absolutely regular. The syllable
count is the same in each corresponding line. The accents fall
where they will.

    The result is a different, triumphantly individual poetry. Her sen-
sibility is meticulous and delicate. She thinks her way through her
subject with deliberate care, which her unexpected breaks reinforce
with prickly insistence. The poems often start with an animal or a
natural creature—although she has poems on steamrollers, baseball players, and a variety of abstract ideas as well—and then move
to unexpected conclusions.

> The Fish
> wade
>
> through black jade.
>   Of the crow-blue mussel shells, one keeps
>   adjusting the ash heaps;
>   opening and shutting itself like
> an
> injured fan.

    The precise picture presented of sea life is then contrasted to
the cliff that it lives against. If the manner is precise, the images
clear, and the form suited to the topic (waves rushing in and out),
the conclusion of the poem, not included above, is ambiguous and
teasingly resists final understanding. The cliff "can live / on what
can not revive / its youth. The sea grows old in it."

    No one has conclusively explained these lines, and the resis-
tance of the poem to final interpretation is another way in which
the poem insists on being itself and not a "statement." It is part of
Moore's irreducibility—the idea that the poem cannot be reduced
to other words or to paraphrase. Her most famous poem, "Poetry,"
("I, too, dislike it . . .") elaborates this idea. The speaker affirms
actuality: "the raw material of poetry in / all its rawness and / that
which is on the other hand / genuine." Where Pound confounds his
readers with a breadth of knowledge, Moore confounds hers with
complex involutions of thought.

2. The Lost Generation

The final description of the men and women who experienced the horrors of World War I and came out of it shaken—having lost their faith in government, God, and most of their peers and elders—was provided by Gertrude Stein. In the epigraph to his first novel *The Sun Also Rises,* Hemingway quotes Stein as saying, "You are all a LOST GENERATION." Hemingway did not reveal the circumstances of Stein's remark, but the term stuck.

H. L. Mencken (1880–1956) and Sinclair Lewis (1885–1951)

The "lost generation" did not apply only to artists and writers. It applied to all Americans who, after the war, found life in the United States to be shallow, empty, vulgar, and unfulfilling. Two famous writers of the time reinforced these beliefs, even if these spokesmen were not themselves part of the "lost generation": H. L. Mencken and Sinclair Lewis.

H[enry] L[ouis] Mencken was an essayist, editor, journalist, and critic, associated with the newspaper *The Baltimore Sun* and two magazines, *The Smart Set* and *The American Mercury,* which he established in 1924. Terming the American middle class, or bourgeoisie, the "booboisie," Mencken, in a series of editorials, opinion pieces, and book reviews, criticized American beliefs and sensibilities.

Mencken's and others' criticisms hit home when, in 1919, the Women's Christian Temperance Union finally succeeded in getting the United States to ratify a constitutional ban on alcohol (PROHIBITION). The sale of liquor was illegal in America after January 15, 1920. In the 1920s in the United States, it was possible to buy liquor from BOOTLEGGERS. The government that legislated this behavior looked as foolish as Mencken and others claimed.

Mencken's most important protégé was the prolific midwestern novelist Sinclair Lewis. In five sharply satirical novels in the 1920s, Lewis presented a sociological survey of America that reached the common reader. *Main Street* (1920) depicted the ignorance and small mindedness—and ultimate triumph—of a small town. *Babbitt* (1922), Lewis's most telling and humorous fiction, skewered the American businessman in the person of an oafish, successful real estate agent who catches a glimpse of a less restricted life but is forced back into the mindless status quo with which he began. *Arrowsmith* (1925) showed that even science can be corrupted.

Elmer-Gantry (1927), the most shocking of Lewis's novels, portrays a hypocritical preacher whose real devotion is to liquor, sex, and money. *Dodsworth* (1929) tells the story of a large-minded business magnate who finds, in Europe, the woman he should have married instead of his superficial wife.

Both Mencken and Lewis were ICONOCLASTS, "idol breakers." Iconodasm was characteristic of the era and of the generation Stein characterized as lost; it had no idols left. The idols of American life—small town goodness, the common man's righteousness, faith in business and religion—Mencken and Lewis broke; the war broke the rest.

F. Scott Fitzgerald (1896–1940)

Curiously, the figure who has come to represent the 1920s as a whole never saw combat in World War I. His fiction is read now with an avidity and admiration it rarely received in his lifetime, and his personal history has become one of the great American stories: F. Scott Fitzgerald.

> ■ ■ **THE QUOTABLE** ■ ■
> **H. L. MENCKEN**
>
> The writer H. L. Mencken was known for his witty one-liners. Here are just a few of his most quotable remarks:
>
> *Any man who afflicts the human race with ideas must be prepared to see them misunderstood.*
>
> *Criticism is prejudice made plausible.*
>
> *It is even harder for the average ape to believe that he has descended from man.*
>
> *Love is the triumph of imagination over intelligence.*
>
> *No one in this world, so far as I know . . . has ever lost money by underestimating the intelligence of the great masses of the plain people.*
>
> *Conscience is the inner voice which warns us that somebody may be looking.*

A Minnesotan who came east for schooling, Fitzgerald fell in love with women whom he idolized and led a chaotic, irresponsible existence. Eventually, he fell in love with an unstable, brilliant, eccentric southern beauty named Zelda Sayre who married him once the publishing firm of Charles Scribner's Sons bought his novel *This Side of Paradise* (1920). A coming-of-age story, *This Side of Paradise* is callow and pretentious, but its hero's attitudes are so close to those of Fitzgerald's peers that it is a faithful recapitulation of the period.

After a second novel, some memorable stories, and an abortive attempt to make money writing a play, Fitzgerald moved to France. There he wrote the novel by which his name lives.

The Great Gatsby (1925)

The doubleness of Fitzgerald's personality melds successfully in this short novel, the subject of which is the American dream: the rise from poverty to wealth and the winning of a love.

Nick Carraway, from the Midwest, tells of coming east and meeting the fabulously high-living and mysteriously wealthy Jay Gatsby, who is in love with Nick's cousin, Daisy Buchanan. Daisy is married and Gatsby tries unsuccessfully to wrest her from her husband.

In the course of these efforts, Gatsby is killed. The novel hints that Gatsby has made his money bootlegging and, possibly, trading in stolen securities. Repelled and saddened, Nick leaves the East to return to the Midwest. The book closes with Nick's mournful, ecstatic meditation on America and its promises.

The Great Gatsby as an American Work

The Great Gatsby is about all of America. Nick Carraway's journey from the Midwest takes him from the heartland to the economic capital of New York. Except for Tom, who is already wealthy, everyone is "on the make," ambitious for money. Gatsby is making money and helping others do so—admittedly in illegal ways, but in ways that the culture supports. The stockbrokers, theatrical and motion picture people, sports figures, tobacco importers, and the like Gatsby entertains represent a cross-section of the wealthy and those eager to be so.

It is a materialistic, consumer culture. Like a hero of one of Horatio Alger's novels—stories of the nineteenth century that

■ ■ **LEWIS, THE ICONOCLAST** ■ ■

Sinclair Lewis's irreverence made him a folk hero to some in the 1920s. He came from Sauk Centre, Minnesota, grew up in stultifying circumstances, and managed what few people ever do: to see the limitations of his environment even while living in it. It gave him a certain freedom of thought and speech. Throughout his "life of noisy desperation" (in Mark Schorer's ironic phrase), he said, drunk or sober, what he thought. Invited to the Bread Loaf Writer's Conference, Lewis asked his audience, "How many of you want to be writers?" Lots of hands went up. "Then why aren't you home writing?" And he stalked off the stage.

Toward the end of his life, in Florence, Italy, a pompous snob of the sort Lewis could not abide lectured his dinner guests at an official reception. "There are two things I do not permit in my presence. One is swearing. The second is addressing me by my first name, which only my mother and Winston Churchill use." On hearing this, Lewis seized his wine glass and yelled, "George, where the hell is the john in this place?"

Iconoclasm was bred deep within.

■ ■ ■ ■ Fitzgerald and the Jazz Age ■ ■ ■ ■ ■

The commercial success of his first novel enabled F. Scott and Zelda Fitzgerald to live in a riotous, extravagant fashion. His short stories sold to high-paying magazines. He bought Zelda a $600 platinum watch at a time when annual salaries of $1,800 were common. Stories of his wild escapades and drinking parties circulated. Whether he and Zelda really did ride down Fifth Avenue on the top of a taxi is uncertain, but he did jump, out of sudden enthusiasm, into the fountain of the Plaza Hotel. And he drank hard, at a time when drinking was considered smart and drinking more considered smarter. He was the living embodiment of the Jazz Age.

His complicated nature always reasserted itself. Although in 1922 he was already dependent on alcohol, he was not yet the troubled alcoholic he would become, and he was indelibly a writer. When he abstained, he wrote. Although his second novel, *The Beautiful and Damned* (1922), is in some ways less controlled than his first, it does go deeper into the lives of its characters, really Zelda and himself, whom he portrayed as increasingly irresponsible and dissipated. He produced three short stories during his early period that, in their own way, are masterpieces: "Bernice Bobs Her Hair," a slight but perfect tale of high spirits; "May Day," a long story about the effects of World War I on members of his own generation, the socialistic philosophies it encouraged, and personal failures it abetted; and "The Diamond as Big as the Ritz," a fantasy set in Montana that explores, exaggerates, and satirizes the lives of the extremely wealthy. These latter two were collected in 1922 in his second collection of short stories, *Tales of the Jazz Age*.

inspired countless Americans to strive and succeed in commerce—Gatsby is a self-made man, springing from "his Platonic conception of himself," beholden to no one. Other characters in the book are trying to emulate him, but they lack his drive and largeness of vision.

The girl he wants is presented in terms that make her pure and alluring. Daisy is charming, she dresses in white, lives in a white house, wears a white dress, has a white car—even her name is that of a white flower, and her maiden name is "Fay" ("fey" meaning "fairy-like"). At the same time as the book sparkles with all this allure and energy, it shows the other side. Daisy is petulant and shallow; she is prepared to betray her husband, who has been unfaithful to her. Her appeal is on the surface. Without reducing

■ ■ ■ ■ Gangsters ■ ■ ■ ■

Since there have been laws, there has been crime. In the 1920s the usual criminal activities of robbery, prostitution, and illegal buying and selling of drugs went on, as did smuggling; to these was added the crime of making and selling illegal liquor. This crime was different from those others, however, because it was condoned in polite society. As a result, some gangsters were not seen as criminals so much as folk heroes of sorts, a fact that lies behind the acceptability of Gatsby in Fitzgerald's novel.

Perhaps the most famous and ruthless gangster was Al[phonse] "Scarface" Capone (1899–1947). Capone ran brothels, numbers rackets (gambling), and anything else that would pay. He was utterly ruthless. The most renowned instance of this was his murder in February 1929 of a rival gang belonging to fellow Chicago gangster, Bugs Moran. By a ruse Capone induced seven members of Moran's organization into a warehouse where his henchmen gunned them all down. Known as the St. Valentine's Day Massacre, it added to Capone's legend. Capone was never convicted of this or any other murder that he organized. Instead, the government imprisoned him for income tax evasion in 1931.

Like Capone, many gangsters then and now had colorful nicknames: Jack "Legs" Diamond, "Samoots" Amatuna, Tony "Ducks" Salerno, Johnny "Behind-the-Deuce" O'Rourke, and, recently, John Gotti, "The Teflon Don."

his glamour, the book shows that Gatsby is a crook and a liar. The people at his parties are drunken, vulgar ingrates. The American dream seemingly can be attained only by compromising the ideals that make it worth pursuing.

In the final pages of the novel, the sweep of American history is alluded to in the landscape itself, as Nick is about to leave Long Island. The fresh, virginal country that "Dutch sailors" first saw is evoked, reinforcing the magic of the American promise. This promise has been tragically betrayed. It is too late, now. The ideals that give meaning to American life are illusions, but Americans strive for them anyway and doing so gives them tragic grandeur.

Its form, its satisfying complexity, its deft selection of detail, its great natural appeal, and its concision make *The Great Gatsby* one of the definitive statements of the American myth.

Fitzgerald after *Gatsby*

The writer of *The Great Gatsby* was at the top of his form. His following collection of short stories contained some his most famous, all associated with *Gatsby:* "Winter Dreams," "Absolution," and "The Rich Boy." Fitzgerald was busy in other ways, too, helping an up-and-coming Hemingway in his career. "It was a time of 1000 parties and no work," he wrote to his editor Maxwell Perkins.

Exiled in Paris, Fitzgerald tried, not always successfully, to resist the parties and write his next novel. Two trips home and abroad again to the Riviera in the south of France occurred before he was able to write for an extended period. During this time, Fitzgerald's life changed. His wife, diagnosed with schizophrenia, was in and out of mental institutions and Fitzgerald's drinking increased.

Pulling from these desperate struggles two of his best short stories, "One Trip Abroad" and "Babylon Revisited," Fitzgerald supported himself by selling fiction to his steadiest market, *The Saturday Evening Post.* At last in 1934 *Tender Is the Night* appeared. The book, the tragic story of a psychiatrist who marries one of his patients but loses her as he sinks into alcoholic depression, succeeded but not to the extent he had hoped. This second great novel was to be Fitzgerald's last. After the modest success and relative failure of his longest collection of short stories, *Taps at Reveille* (1935), Fitzgerald sank into debt and alcoholism.

In the midst of writing what promised to be a first-rate novel about Hollywood, *The Love of the Last Tycoon* (or *The Last Tycoon*), his years of indulgence caught up with Fitzgerald. He died, age 44, his novel half finished.

Ernest Hemingway (1899–1961)

Fitzgerald's personal fame diminished even as his abilities as a writer increased, and his friend Ernest Hemingway followed a complementary path. In the first half of the twentieth century, Hemingway became the most famous American writer in the world. Once the embodiment of the lost generation, Hemingway was not only a great writer but also a great sportsman and a great drinker, a man of discipline who understood how to enjoy life to the fullest. No one could live up to the HEMINGWAY MYTH, not even the man himself. However, the early Hemingway was a great writer. More than two dozen short stories and several novels attest to his power and originality. He was a formulaic writer. A definable code underlies his work, but unlike his inferiors and his imitators, which in the 1940s and 1950s were many, it is his own code; the

The Charleston in Washington, D.C.
In the 1920s, no part of the country was immune
from jaunty irreverence and the flapper—the young
devil-may-care female of the period. Here two women
do the famous dance in full view of Representative
T.S. McMillan of South Carolina and other lawmakers
and politicos.

▪ ▪ ▪ ▪ HEMINGWAY IN HIS TIME ▪ ▪ ▪ ▪

Although his greatest artistic achievements were written before 1934, Hemingway's reputation as a writer increased steadily throughout the 1930s. He appeared on the cover of *Time* magazine in 1937. What about Hemingway appealed so deeply to people of the lost generation?

Like many cultural icons, he was both of his time and apart from it. The despair that T. S. Eliot had set down as early as 1922 and that was a mantra of the 1920s resonates throughout Hemingway's writing. The precision of Hemingway's expression means that this despair is more fully realized there than elsewhere, and the writing, the art, also provides a way out of the despair itself. Doing something well is Hemingway's answer to meaninglessness, and art is the supreme expression of competence. He had found a way.

Moreover, Hemingway's art was not an exclusive affair, not an activity of a person who lives in isolation. However rarefied and special his gifts, Hemingway had nothing of the precious about him. Not only writing but also drinking, fishing, fighting, and making love were activities that in his fiction Hemingway raised to the level of art and imbued with special significance. These activities are done by people who feel they have nothing of the aesthetic in them. In an empty age lost in economic and political ineptness, Hemingway came up with an affirmation.

devices are ones he developed and used effectively because he understood them better than anyone else.

If World War I deprived humanity of its faith and made daily living meaningless and empty, then style—the way in which one lived—becomes all important. The lost generation could not redeem the conditions of existence but it could abide in grace and decency. To a shattered individual, *what* one did mattered less than *how* one did it.

The Short Stories

Three prime examples of shattered persons who follow this code are Nick Adams of *In Our Time* (1925); Jake Barnes, the hero of *The Sun Also Rises* (1926); and Lieutenant Frederic Henry of *A Farewell to Arms* (1929). On a solitary fishing trip in the woods Nick Adams is aware of the dangers surrounding him, which are psychological as well as physical.

Ernest Hemingway with a marlin
This is Hemingway, the legendary sportsman, proud
of a good catch. At times defiantly nonliterary and
never wholly at home among intellectuals ("I was not
made to think," says the hero of *A Farewell to Arms*),
Hemingway liked to mask his aesthetic and intellectual
sophistication.

The prose that describes young Nick Adams (the name "Adams" suggests the first man, but one who has been "nicked" or marred) is deliberately simple. Hemingway picked up this technique from Gertrude Stein. He put it to his own use, imbuing his prose with ominousness. He interspersed the stories in *In Our Time* with brief vignettes that told of the horrors of World War I. Although Hemingway does not make the connections explicit, they are there.

Hemingway's stylistic talents were ideally suited to the short story. The economy and spectacular effects he gained by leaving elements of the plot unsaid resonate beyond and between his sentences. Short stories, such as "The Battler," "The Killers," "Hills Like White Elephants," "A Clean, Well-Lighted Place," "Now I Lay Me," "The Short Happy Life of Francis Macomber," and "The Snows of Kilimanjaro," present worlds of menace and despair in which characters try to exhibit the stoic nobility of people trapped in tragic circumstances.

"Hills Like White Elephants" from *Men Without Women* (1927) exhibits Hemingway's strengths. A woman, Jig, and her lover wait in a Spanish train station for the train to Madrid, where Jig is to undergo an abortion.

The word *abortion* never occurs in the story. The reader is left to understand the situation from the dialogue. This omission, characteristic of Hemingway, makes the procedure seem more terrifying, as though it is more than just the "simple operation" that the man defensively portrays it to be. It is more: It may well be the end of the relationship.

The setting of the story, a bar in a hot part of Spain, is relevant. The dryness and heat around the couple are emblematic of their lack of connection and love. To compensate for this lack, they drink. "That's all we do, isn't it—look at things and try new drinks?" To this question the man can respond only "I guess so." However, drinking is even unsatisfactory in itself. "Everything tastes of licorice. Especially all the things you've waited so long for, like absinthe."

"Hills Like White Elephants" gains additional force through irresolution. After the man drinks some anisette he sees people "waiting reasonably for the train." This ordinary life is something far distant from him at the moment. When he returns to Jig to continue waiting for the train, she smiles at him and says, in unconscious defensiveness, "I feel fine. . . . There's nothing wrong with me. I feel fine." Told in a flat, reportorial style, the story is as unresolved as the relationship it depicts. The male gives no sign of impatience;

■ ■ ■ ■ ■ HEMINGWAY AND THE MARKET ■ ■ ■ ■ ■
FOR SHORT STORIES

The market for short stories in the 1920s was much more active than it is today. Many mass-circulation magazines, such as *The Saturday Evening Post, Redbook*, and *The Metropolitan*, published eight or more short stories in a single issue, whereas now most mass-circulation periodicals devote an equal or greater space to articles and nonfiction. In the 1920s short stories paid very well, and at his peak F. Scott Fitzgerald could earn $4,000 for a single story. This was at a time when some families were living on half of that for an entire year.

Interestingly enough, Ernest Hemingway never entered the world of high-paying short story writing, although it was his short stories as much as his novels that made him famous. Hemingway published in smaller-circulation, more exclusively aesthetic magazines, such as *Scribner's* (owned by his publisher, Charles Scribner's Sons); *The Little Review*, which also once published parts of Joyce's *Ulysses*; and, sometimes, *The Atlantic Monthly*. Simple sales did not interest him as much as artistic excellence. Later on, however, Hemingway did write for *Esquire* magazine, then considered somewhat risqué, a "man's magazine." Two of his greatest short stories, "The Short Happy Life of Francis Macomber" and "The Snows of Kilimanjaro," appeared in *Esquire*.

By the late 1930s, when he brought out his collected short stories, Hemingway's interest in the form had died. Although editors, such as Harold Ross of *The New Yorker*, asked Hemingway for contributions, he had nothing to send.

he bears his burden with a certain heroic stoicism that does not wholly condone him, as his own responses leave Jig more or less on her own in a situation he also created.

The Novels

Heroic stoicism could be judged a quality of Hemingway's two most famous novels, *The Sun Also Rises* and *A Farewell to Arms*. Jake Barnes, the hero of the former, is in love with Lady Brett Ashley, a hard-drinking, high-spirited, at-loose-ends Englishwoman. Prevented from consummating their relationship by a wound, the nature of which the novel does not specify, he watches her drift through a series of unsatisfactory relationships with other men from among their shiftless, artistic acquaintances. He takes such satisfaction as he can from a fishing trip in the mountains of Spain and from watching bullfights, a sport whose ritualized violence and exactness releases him by reenacting the grim conditions of existence.

An even greater popular success followed with *A Farewell to Arms* (1929). It is a love story. In *The Sun Also Rises* love between Jake Barnes and Brett Ashley was impossible. Lieutenant Frederick Henry, an American attached to an Italian unit, can make love. During an idyllic summer, nurse Catherine Barkley becomes pregnant by him.

As Hemingway aged, his heroes became simpler and more besieged, his women less individualized. The ritualistic pleasures—the sports and the drinking—gave way in the 1930s to a tentatively asserted but not fully explored socialism in *To Have and Have Not* (1937) and *For Whom the Bell Tolls* (1940).

By 1940, Hemingway had said what he had to say. In 1950 he published *Across the River and into the Trees,* a book on which critics heaped scorn. The hero, a World War I veteran named Colonel Cantwell, is in love with a very young woman whom he calls "daughter." The rituals in violence and sports that in earlier books staved off despair here involve opening bottles of champagne and sitting in restaurants.

Hemingway achieved a comeback of sorts with *The Old Man and the Sea* (1952), a NOVELLA about an old Cuban fisherman who catches an extraordinary marlin only to have it eaten by sharks before he can bring it home. A classroom staple and a best seller, this last book was responsible for his reaping the prizes rightfully his for work he had done years previous. After two disastrous plane crashes and more hard living, Hemingway deteriorated. In 1961 in his home in Ketchum, Idaho, at the height of his fame, he committed suicide.

Hemingway's techniques and his advice on writing continue to influence practitioners of fiction. His practice of always stopping before he had truly finished in order to know where to begin when he resumed has influenced many writers. His principle of never interfering in the story became practically universal. Hemingway's fiction avoids conscious authorial intervention. Finally his style, perhaps the most recognizable one in twentieth century writing, and his focus on letting the story speak for itself were hugely influential. It was not until the advent of postmodernism in the 1960s and 1970s that Hemingway's influence began to fade.

3. Modernism in the American Novel: Joyce, Dos Passos, and Faulkner

The techniques that Eliot, Stein, and others brought to verse were also brought to fiction. Collage, associative thinking, verbal play for the sake of pattern, and bold experimentation characterize modernism in the novel. Just as any discussion of modernism in general has to deal with the central moral text of modern times, *The Waste Land,* any discussion of modernism in the novel has to take into account the central fictional work of the modernist period, James Joyce's *Ulysses,* published in the same year as Eliot's poem. More than any other writer, Joyce (1882–1941), an Irishman, changed modern fiction. His work is central to modernism. It introduced in full realized form the techniques of modernist fiction. It was read by Dos Passos, Hemingway, Fitzgerald, Faulkner—by every serious writer after 1922.

James Joyce's *Ulysses* (1922)

Ulysses is less of a novel with an evident plot line than a presentation of human existence through a variety of literary techniques. The entire book, over 700 pages, takes place in Dublin on June 16, 1904, and concerns the wanderings of two men in that city. Throughout the course of that day, one or the other of them and sometimes both go to public baths and a newspaper office, attend a funeral, and visit various places: the library, pubs, a maternity hospital, a brothel.

As they wander, Joyce dips into the minds of these characters and into the minds of others whom they meet. He attempts to present their innermost thoughts, seemingly without editing or any device that would interfere with what they are thinking; this is the well-known technique of STREAM OF CONSCIOUSNESS.

At the same time as this is occurring, the story implicitly compares the meanderings to those of Odysseus, the hero of Homer's *Odyssey.* One episode might correspond to the famous encounter between Odysseus (Ulysses in Latinized form) and Polyphemos, the Cyclops; another parallels Odysseus's encounter with the goddess Circe; still another focuses—with broad irony—on Penelope, Odysseus's wife.

James Joyce, the author, disapproved of contrivance, the way novels depend upon coincidence and forcing events to fit a shaped plot; he also felt that such fiction could not adequately represent

. . . . THE ODYSSEY . . . .

The story behind *Ulysses* is one of the oldest stories known. After the ten-year Trojan War, an event that actually occurred around 1250 B.C. but was not set down by Homer until some 500 years afterward, one of the greatest of Greek heroes, Ulysses (the Roman version of the Greek name Odysseus), was left to find his way back to his native island of Ithaca. The gods and goddesses had other plans for him, and he had many adventures on his voyage homeward. He encountered monsters and natural hardships; he was forced to serve two mistresses—Circe and Calypso—and he several times had to turn down offers of marriage.

Eventually, however, he does arrive home where he finds that his wife Penelope has been faithful, putting off suitors who want to marry her for the family money. He enters his own hall disguised as a beggar and with the help of his faithful son Telemachus turns the tables on those who would plunder his house, killing them before being reunited with his wife.

For Joyce, Ulysses was the complete man: thinker, actor, husband, lover, farmer, warrior, earthy and noble at once. He finds some of these same qualities, in comically changed form, in the hero of his novel *Ulysses*, Leopold Bloom, a Dublin Jew who sells advertising. In conflating the stories of Bloom and Ulysses, Joyce joins the modern world to the ancient one.

the comically bewildering variety of the experience of life itself. Believing in little except the power of the human mind to recreate experience, Joyce wanted to present that experience naturally, without interference, but at the same time to enrich it, as Eliot and Pound did, through parallels with myth and through the shapeliness and control of art. Like Freud, Joyce was not afraid to deal explicitly with sexual matters, although the myth he chose was not that of Oedipus but of Odysseus; like Freud, Joyce was censored, and it was not until 1934 that Americans could legally buy and read *Ulysses*. The exiles in Paris, however, in Gertrude Stein's salon or the expatriate circles all knew the novel.

Revolutionary, allusive, learned, subtle, funny, *Ulysses* made such a complete and authoritative rejection of conventional fiction that afterward previous ways of writing seemed quaint. Not easy to read, it changed writing permanently. The old fiction was limited, perhaps dead. Even novelists apart from Joyce's circle, who did not remain in Paris or never were exiles there, were affected by it. Two of the most prominent of these were John Dos Passos and William Faulkner.

John Dos Passos (1896–1970)

There is no clearer illustration of the effect of Joyce on the writing of fiction than the works of John Dos Passos. The difference shows clearly between Dos Passos's first two novels—*One Man's Initiation* (1917) and *Three Soldiers* (1921)—and his breakthrough novel *Manhattan Transfer* (1925). *Three Soldiers* is a conventional novel. The reader follows the vagaries of three protagonists with interest, and there is a nicely balanced feel to the presentation. Dos Passos's contempt for inhumanity and the waste of war is palpable, and the story's full, rounded, self-contained plot neatly contrasts the sensitive Harvard graduate to the dull conformist. It ends poignantly. But it pales beside *Manhattan Transfer.*

This is another kind of book altogether. Whereas the center of *Three Soldiers* is clearly indicated by its title, *Manhattan Transfer* has many centers, with eight major characters, more or less, and six others briefly sketched on the side. It loosely intertwines their lives. The cover of the first edition, with the author's painting of Manhattan on it, suggests the explosion of energy in the prose. Joyce-like but not Joycean, *Manhattan Transfer* bursts on the reader in a kaleidoscope of styles. It moves back and forth through time but is largely set in the 1920s. It is part straight narration, part NATURALISM in the style of Theodore Dreiser—detailed reportage with no authorial intervention—and part dizzying impressionism with fragmented descriptions that give the feel of the situation without detailed specifics. For short bursts, it is Joycean stream-of-consciousness, and everywhere studded with slangy dialogue, French, and snatches of songs. The book presents New York as a metropolis of ambitious, corrupt businessmen and show people, where luck betrays and rarely rewards, and, for all the frenetic riotousness, fails to satisfy.

It is the most detail- and incident-jammed, exhilarating novel in American letters. Although the book looks forbidding and strange, the reader is drawn in, and Dos Passos uses the time-tested narrative technique of breaking off episodes at the height of their interest to start a new one—which is then broken off. Through it all, the reader is moved, compelled.

Dos Passos's most extended triumph in this mode is a set of three novels: *The 42nd Parallel* (1930), *1919* (1932), and *The Big*

Money (1936). He eventually collected them into one large book of more than 1,000 pages titled *U.S.A.* This long trilogy presents America from 1905 to 1935, with a number of actual historical characters appearing.

As in *Manhattan Transfer,* the lives of the characters intersect. The brother of Janey Williams, who meets the newspaper owner and sharp trader J. Ward Moorehouse in *The 42nd Parallel,* is the brother of the Joe Williams whose ship is blown up in *1919.* J. Ward Moorehouse, with whom Janey Williams has an affair, gives one Richard Ellsworth Savage a job in his public relations firm. A girl he impregnates is killed, preserving his chances of advancement at the Moorehouse firm. In *The Big Money,* Savage continues to make connections among the powerful. Plainly, he will step into the shoes of his boss at the Moorehouse PR firm.

This is to pick three brief strands from three full-length novels. There are many other characters—industrialists, failed and successful businessmen, aspiring actresses, Communist organizers, reporters, printers, hobos, labor leaders, chorus girls, strikers, and strikebreakers.

Invented characters are not the only ones in *U.S.A.* Famous personalities come in as well: Eugene V. Debs, the socialist labor leader and five-time presidential candidate; Luther Burbank, the horticulturalist; Andrew Carnegie, the steel magnate; the Wright brothers; Frank Lloyd Wright, the architect; the dancer Isadora Duncan; William Randolph Hearst, the newspaper tycoon; Rudolph Valentino, the actor; Henry Ford, the automobile manufacturer; President Theodore Roosevelt; the poet and journalist John Reed; and even the Unknown Soldier are there. Dos Passos, in modernist style, blurs the line between created fiction and reality. It's all real, or all made-up, and it all connects.

Set forth in distinct typographic display, two other deliberate facets of the novel, aside from invented lives and real lives, assault the eye of the reader. Dos Passos calls the first of these "newsreels." These are headlines that might appear in any newspaper of the time followed by distillations of stories, excerpts from popular songs, sentences cut from wire dispatches, a collage of items that recall the times not for the sake of nostalgia but to give the events of the ordinary characters a dignity the media miss and to put the reader there.

(from 1919) Newsreel XX
Oh the infantree the infantree

■ ■ ■ ■ NEWSREELS IN DOS PASSOS'S NOVELS ■ ■ ■ ■

Two strategies lie behind Dos Passos's interspersing his stories with "news-reels." The first is to give them the force, authority, and modernity of the short news features shown before full-length films in motion picture houses. Before television, when only some households in America had radio receivers, newsreels were the means of supplementing newspapers in keeping Americans informed about the world around them.

This, Dos Passos is saying, is what is happening in America as its own press reports it. There is no interference or interpretation.

The second strategy, deriving from the first, is to blend, in modernist fashion, different genres. In order to create a populist literature, a goal at which *U.S.A.* is aiming, there is a direct link between events and so-called fiction.

The typographic distinctiveness of the newsreels in *U.S.A.* is supplemented by other sections, placed close to them, called "The Camera Eye." Set in larger type more widely spaced, "The Camera Eye" is Dos Passos's equivalent of the collective stream of consciousness. Here is the thinking of the entire nation, what it believes and how it sees the world around it.

In *The ABC of Reading*, Ezra Pound said, famously, "Literature is news that STAYS news." Dos Passos inverts Pound's statement: News is literature that STAYS literature.

With the dirt behind their ears
ARMIES CLASH AT VERDUN IN GLOBE'S
GREATEST BATTLE
150,000 MEN AND WOMEN PARADE

but another question and a very important one is raised. The New York Stock Exchange is today the only free securities market in the world. If it maintains that position it is sure to become the world's greatest center for the marketing of. . . .

Dos Passos's political stance is radical. Like many intellectuals of the 1930s, he was a leftist, more so than Hemingway or Dreiser and certainly more than F. Scott Fitzgerald. Unlike those others, his wide traveling and his refusal to take a regular job for any length

■ ■ ■ ■ COMMUNISM IN AMERICA ■ ■ ■ ■

Communism is a system of government in which the property of the community is owned equally by all. Propounded first by Karl Marx and Frederich Engels in the nineteenth century, the philosophy was first adopted in the Soviet Union after the Russian Revolution in 1917. Its leader, Lenin, urged workers everywhere to overthrow their governments.

During World War I, Americans were on the watch for spies and sabotage in factories. Because many of the unskilled laborers who worked in factories were foreigners, communism and foreigners were feared in the 1920s.

However, when the stock market crashed and thousands of workers lost their jobs in the 1930s, the period known as the Great Depression, many began to revise their thinking about communism and communist ideals. Intellectuals and artists such as Dos Passos openly avowed communist ideas. It is in this context that the *U.S.A.* trilogy and other novels, such as Steinbeck's *Grapes of Wrath*, were composed.

of time, gave him authority. His sympathy for the common person, those out of power, and the downtrodden comes from his having been these things, as well as having been intermittently an acquaintance of the wealthy and the powerful.

The last section of *U.S.A.,* like that of *Manhattan Transfer,* is devoted to "a young man . . . at the edge of the concrete, with . . . a rubbed suitcase of phony leather, the other hand almost making a fist, thumb up." He is a hobo hitching a ride, having come from New York and heading west, repeating, as one who has been rejected by America, the westward journey of America. He is like Huckleberry Finn—"lighting out for the territory ahead of the rest." With all the disaffected feelings of the beat generation and a good deal more concrete social awareness, Dos Passos shaped the epic of the first three decades of the twentieth century in modernist fiction.

William Faulkner (1897–1962)

Many critics judge William Faulkner as the greatest American novelist of the twentieth century. The author of more than two dozen books, he extended the thematic reach of modernism and applied its techniques to new material, allying it to folklore, tall tale, and regionalism. Stream-of-consciousness technique applied to poor, rural southern characters pervades Faulkner's early fiction. Modernism is everywhere in his blending of nineteenth-century regionalism with experimental fictional technique. Faulkner is a Joycean raised on southern myth, tall tales, obsessive morbidity, and sexual fixation. Inventive genius, flexibility of language, an all-permeating empathy, and sheer intensity make Faulkner's narratives universal. The fiction he wrote from 1928 to 1936 is the kernel of his achievement, although several of his short stories, such as "A Rose for Emily," "That Evening Sun," and "Barn Burning," have become emblems of the work as a whole.

In 1928, using the stream-of-consciousness techniques learned from Joyce and emulating Joyce's example of following his own bent irrespective of what a reader might expect, Faulkner wrote the first of his five great novels: *The Sound and the Fury.* This book, which makes no concessions to popular expectation, is divided into four sections, each with a different narrator. The title, from *Macbeth* ("Life's but a walking shadow, a poor player / That struts and frets his hour upon the stage, / And then is heard no more. It is a tale / Told by an idiot, full of sound and fury, / Signifying nothing.") literally inspires the first section. Dated April 7, 1928, Chapter 1 is told by an actual idiot, Benjy Compson, born Maury, age 33, a castrate whose mental deficiency is biological evidence of the decline of the Compson family.

Although each section of *The Sound and the* Fury is dated and although April 7 is Benjy's own birthday, for Benjy time does not exist. His reality is a constant present. The cues the reader has that Benjy is remembering are a repeated word and the switch into italic or roman type face and whether the caretaker with him is Versh or Luster, but neither the book nor Benjy makes a distinction between memory and present occurrence.

Benjy's life is unrelieved emotional torture and physical pain. Attracted to a fire, he tries to touch it. His memories center on the person who has treated him most kindly, his promiscuous sister Candace, called Caddy. He associates the young Caddy—she has since left the family—with the smell of trees and grass. Forced to watch Caddy's lovemaking, Benjy misinterprets sex as aggression. In this case the aggression is against his loved object, whose leaving him is intertwined with the memory of her appeal. He is tended in 1928 by a black servant, a boy ironically named Luster, who leads him near a golf course to search for a lost quarter so that he can attend a traveling show. Luster is unaware of Benjy's feelings and that the word "caddie," heard on the golf course, will bring Caddy to Benjy's mind. All this is conveyed in a flat tone that underscores Benjy's lack of self and the separation of others from him.

The second section occurs eighteen years before the first. A stylistic contrast, it is told by Benjy's brother Quentin, a Harvard student. Unlike Benjy, Quentin is preoccupied with time. Shadows, clocks and watches, and death dominate his thinking, as does an obsession with virginity, in particular that of his sister, Caddy, the mother of a daughter also named Quentin. Like Benjy, Quentin moves back and forth in time, but the events in his section slide into each other in a way that points to the disintegration of his personality. (Although Benjy can communicate nothing, he sees precisely.) Quentin is highly verbal and subtle, but he is unable to order his life successfully. In taking us inside his mind in stream-of-consciousness fashion, Faulkner lets Quentin's confused connections imbue the archetypically southern Compson family with a general sense of defeat. Quentin's story has a tragic end. The date of the telling, June 2, 1910, is the day Quentin commits suicide by jumping from a bridge in Cambridge, Massachusetts.

After the unrelieved tragedy of the first two sections, the third is full of mean-spirited comedy. The date is April 6, 1928. Narrated by the brother of Benjy and Quentin, Jason, who works as a clerk in a store, the events are told in straightforward fashion, but the clarity is less of a relief than it might be, for Jason is shallower than either of his brothers, and his comedy has its own place in the tragedy of the Compson family. Funny though he is, Jason is cruel and selfish. He lies, steals money from his mother, is prejudiced against Italians and Jews, gratuitously burns circus tickets that he

> ■　■ THE SOUND AND THE FURY ■　■
> Literary critic Malcolm Cowley, who knew Faulkner well, offered this shrewd, droll description of his friend's writing.
>
> *The truth is that Faulkner unites in his work two of the dominant trends in American literature from the beginning: that of the psychological horror story as developed by Hawthorne, Poe, and Stephen Crane, among others; and that of realistic frontier humor, with Mark Twain as its best example. If you imagine Huckleberry Finn living in the House of Usher and telling uproarious stories while the walls crumble about him, that will give you the double quality of Faulkner's work at its best.*
>
> In Otis E. Wheeler's "Some Uses of Folk Humor in Faulkner," in F.W. Wagner, ed., *William Faulkner, Four Decades of Criticism.*

**William Faulkner photo taken in 1954
by the American photographer Carl Van
Vechten (1880–1964)**
This is the older, more public Faulkner, nattily
dressed, having won the Nobel Prize, the author
of *A Fable*.

■ ■ ■ ■ FAULKNER IN HOLLYWOOD ■ ■ ■ ■

A fiercely private man, an alcoholic, and an avid hunter, Faulkner lived for years from hand to mouth, unable until his last decade to earn a secure living from his books. Like many writers, he turned to Hollywood, which he disliked, for high-paying writing jobs but even there manifested a cranky, even scornful independence. Once, when a producer gave him permission to finish writing a screenplay at home, away from the studio, Faulkner decided that home meant Oxford, Mississippi, so he took his work back there.

Nor would he be patronized. Hunting with the actor and star of *Gone with the Wind*, Clark Gable, a very well-known figure in his day, Faulkner mentioned one of his novels. "Ah," said Gable, "you write then, Mr. Faulkner?" "Yes. And what is it you do, Mr. Gable?"

doesn't want but that Luster does, and steals the money Quentin (Caddy's daughter, named after her uncle) sends her mother in order to finance his own failing cotton speculations and to sustain the woman he calls his mistress, a prostitute named Lorraine. "I never promise a woman anything nor let her know what I'm going to give her," he explains. "That's the only way to manage them. Always keep them guessing. If you can't think of any other way to surprise them, give them a bust in the jaw." He hates Caddy and tells her she would be better off with Quentin, that is, dead. He calls Benjy "The Great American Gelding."

The first three sections of *The Sound and the Fury* are told by confused, unreliable narrators. The last is told in the third person. It centers on the Compsons' cook, Luster's grandmother, Dilsey, who serves the erratic, irrational Compsons without complaining. It is Easter morning. Dilsey attends church. Unlike her employers, Dilsey is focused on the life to come, not the past. But that past seems to repeat itself when Jason discovers that his niece Quentin has run away and robbed what he considers his strongbox, which contains the money he has been pilfering. Weighed down by past memories, Mrs. Compson, Jason's mother, thinks that her granddaughter Quentin has committed suicide like her son of the same name.

Bold and experimental as *The Sound and Fury* is, Faulkner had not finished his modernist experimentations. His succeeding novel, *As I Lay Dying,* has no third-person narration. Instead, fifteen

different narrators tell the story. The dirt-poor Bundren family—
Cash, Darl, Jewel, Vardaman, and Dewey Dell and their father
Anse—want to journey to Jefferson to bury their matriarch, Addie
Bundren, who lies dying and in fact does die shortly after the story
opens. Faulkner's ability to move the narrative forward coherently
and to enter the minds of many distinctively varied narrators makes
this short novel a tour de force, a spectacular demonstration of
Faulkner's skill as a writer. Moreover, unlike *The Sound and the
Fury* and other modernist fictions, no final truth emerges from *As I
Lay Dying*. The character who seems closest to knowing the truth
and who is the most reliable is institutionalized. The moments of
tenderness and pain, insensitivity and cruelty, that the family experiences are balanced in a way that makes them, poor and primitive
as they are, a mirror for all that human beings do to one another
and the story a paradigm for all of life. The modernist technique
dramatizes the essential isolation of human beings locked within
themselves, only intermittently connecting with each other.

After these two remarkable novels, Faulkner wrote at least
three others at the same level of achievement: *Sanctuary* (1931),
Light in August (1932), and *Absalom, Absalom!* (1936). The last of
these, in which modernism seems pushed almost as far as it can
go, is also a GOTHIC NOVEL.

The Sound and the Fury and *As I Lay Dying* show the different realities of distinctly different narrators. In *Absalom, Absalom!*
this theme is to the fore and presented in a new way. *Absalom,
Absalom!* tells one story, already over before the telling begins,
from three perspectives: those of Rosa Coldfield, Mr. Compson—
the father of Quentin Compson from *The Sound and the Fury*—and
then in a reinvented form by Quentin himself, talking to his Harvard
roommate Shreve. It is the account of a man named Thomas Sut-
pen who in 1833 arrives in Jefferson, Mississippi, and creates for
himself a southern version of the American dream.

Although each of the narrators in *The Sound and the Fury*
and *As I Lay Dying* is clearly delineated, in *Absalom, Absalom!* the
voices blend into a whole, sustained only by the telling of the story,
which is once again the subject of the book. As with Joyce, it is
language that dominates, language that in *Absalom, Absalom!* is
"that meager and fragile thread . . . by which the little surface cor-
ners and edges of men's secret and solitary lives may be joined
for an instant now and then before sinking back into the darkness
where the spirit cried for the first time and was not heard and will
cry for the last time and will not be heard either." This pessimistic

▪ ▪ ▪ ▪ FAULKNER ON FAULKNER ▪ ▪ ▪ ▪
"I'm just a farmer who likes to tell stories."

Faulkner was fond of downplaying his sophistication and intelligence with remarks such as that, but part of him found the seriousness with which his novels were read amusing and off-putting. He was a thoroughly modern man, at home in the most sophisticated of literary circles, but novelists are also entertainers, wanting to make their readers laugh and feel moved and willing to use every device necessary to achieve those ends. At the height of his inventiveness, Faulkner's novels used all the tricks of the moderns, although, as one reader noted, *The Sound and the Fury* at its core is like a Victorian novel: It is about the same things with which nineteenth-century novels were concerned—the decline of the family, money, orphans, death and decay, and social conflict. So maybe, in addition to being an avant-garde writer, Faulkner was, after all, just a farmer who liked to tell stories.

perspective, this isolation is reinforced by the lack of chronology and connectivity of the plot and the apparently rambling quality of Faulkner's style, where the sentences stream out of consciousness to carry the reader along so that the book seems a tissue of words set against the sensual details that the narrators involuntarily evoke, as though repeating the futile gesture were the only exercise open to a man (or woman) in a life filled with remorse and self-contained angst.

Faulkner's courage in confronting racial issues and his refusal to compromise his aesthetic aims set an example for novelists to come. He liberated writers and provided release and pleasure to readers willing to follow his powerful, convoluted narratives.

4. The Harlem Renaissance (1919–1929)

Harlem was originally a Dutch settlement in the area above what is now midtown Manhattan in New York. During the early years of World War I (1914–1918) it came to be settled by black people—some of them natural American citizens from the South, others from other countries.

The Great Migration was on. The term was originally applied in the seventeenth century to the exodus of people from England to Massachusetts. In the 1920s the Great Migration referred to the exodus of African Americans from the South to Chicago and cities in the North. They were seeking better jobs. While many worked in positions as menial and deadening as those they had left, some did not, and they found themselves in a new environment. The sudden influx of blacks, the energy derived from a change of scenery, and the celebratory mood of the country ignited a burst of creativity. It amounted to a movement and was called the Harlem Renaissance.

The Harlem Renaissance was not only a literary phenomenon. Musicians, actors, and actresses became stars playing for black and white audiences. Sometimes performers toured, as performers do today, but sometimes they worked exclusively in Harlem. Whites took taxis into Harlem to be entertained by such performers as Louis Armstrong, Bessie Smith, Duke Ellington, Ethel Waters, and Paul Robeson, who, by the end of the 1920s, were nationally known figures.

> ## ▪ ▪ WHITE LANDLORDS, ▪ ▪ BLACK TENANTS
>
> Harlem accommodated blacks because the whites who owned buildings could make a handsome profit. Richard Wright, in *12 Million Black Voices,* detailed how the system worked. A seven-room apartment that rented to whites for $50 a month was spliced into seven tiny units. Each was rented to a black family for $6 a week. Thus, real estate that had been bringing in $50 a month now earned $168 if it was fully occupied.
>
> Whites may have been benefiting, but blacks benefited too. "Negro was in vogue," wrote Langston Hughes, and many African Americans, wanting to be where the action was, were glad of the chance to live in Harlem. The population of the area doubled from 1900 to 1920, and by 1930 there were, according to James Weldon Johnson in *Black Manhattan*, 200,000 people living in Harlem. The result of this cultural explosion was that Harlem was no longer a ghetto; it had become a distinctly black city. What began as exploitation evolved into something else.

▪ ▪ ▪ ▪ SPEAKEASIES ▪ ▪ ▪ ▪

Prohibition was simply impossible to enforce. People who wanted to drink in bars found ways to do so that almost openly flouted the law. One method was the club called a "speakeasy." This was an establishment, advertised only by word of mouth, where people could gather to drink. In many cases, one could gain entrance to a speakeasy by the use of a password. A patron would knock on the door and a small partition would be pulled back. "Joe sent me," was sometimes all that was required to gain access.

Renowned bars in New York, such as the Stork Club, later legitimate, started as speakeasies. The subsequently famous 21 Club was another, and it was known for its elaborate mechanical bar designed to fool the police. If the club was raided by authorities, as frequently occurred, the bartender pushed a hidden button and shelves of liquor bottles descended out of view via a dumbwaiter to a secret room in the basement.

Some owners of speakeasies became celebrities. The most renowned was Texas Guinan, a tough-talking businesswoman who is reported to have greeted each patron with the phrase, "Hello, sucker!" That didn't stop people from coming: Texas Guinan made a small fortune during the 1920s.

The theaters and nightclubs—as well as speakeasies, where bootleg liquor was served—were owned by whites, as were the publishing houses that printed the works of the writers associated with the Harlem Renaissance, but the grouping of talent and its cross-pollination, with one art inspiring another, was distinctively black. This was the beginning of an independent and sometimes defiant black culture that insisted on its own values. If Alfred A. Knopf, who published the poetry of Langston Hughes, and the owners of Harper and Brothers, who published Countee Cullen's work, Horace Liveright, who published Jean Toomer's *Cane,* and Alfred Harcourt and Donald Brace, who published Claude McKay's *Harlem Shadows*, were white, they nonetheless purveyed this work to a wider audience than any black ENTREPRENEUR could have done.

Jazz originated as improvisational music played by black bands in the South in the early twentieth century. What F. Scott Fitzgerald had called the Jazz Age and the Harlem Renaissance coincided. In fact, the closest connection between jazz and literature is found in writers of the Harlem Renaissance. The impulse for much writing of the Harlem Renaissance was not, however, purely musical or aesthetic.

It was social and psychological. As Alain Locke, the Howard University philosophy professor, said, writers of the Harlem Renaissance "sense[d] within their group a spiritual wealth which if they [could] properly expound, [would] be ample for a new judgment and reappraisal of the race."

W[illiam] E[dward] B[urghardt] Du Bois (1868–1963)

The great educator, historian, and black leader whose 95-year life spanned from Reconstruction, the period after the Civil War, to the beginning of the Civil Rights movement, was active in literary, social, and intellectual circles during the Harlem Renaissance. Although he published *The Souls of Black Folk* a decade before the movement in Harlem began, his influence continued, and Du Bois regularly reviewed books on African American issues during the 1920s.

A former SOCIALIST still vitally interested in social issues, Du Bois was an important editor. He took over *The Crisis,* the magazine of the National Association for the Advancement of Colored People (NAACP). Living in Harlem and actively promoting interracial understanding, Du Bois founded a black theater group, Krigwa (a word that evolved from the first letters of Crisis Group of Writers and Artists), and began to focus on the place of blacks worldwide. His interest in Africa resulted in an essay "The Negro Minds Reaches Out" in Alain Locke's influential collection, *The New Negro: An Intepretation.*

▪ ▪ GOING UP TO HARLEM ▪ ▪ FOR SOME JAZZ

The impetus for whites to visit Harlem may have begun in 1921 with a Broadway musical called *Shuffle Along.* Midtown Manhattan had never seen an all African American revue, and the popularity of *Shuffle Along* was quickly noted. Imitations followed: *Liza, Chocolate Dandies*, and *Runnin' Wild.*

Attending a Broadway theater was different from being in Harlem, and it soon became clear that there was money to be made from visitors. Soon over 500 jazz places served white patrons who wanted to see what the excitement was about. The best known were the Cotton Club and Connie's Inn. Although ostensibly run by blacks, they were often white owned, sometimes by gangsters, such as George "Big Frenchy" DeMange.

These jazz clubs changed the world of music forever. Duke Ellington and Fletcher Henderson worked in this milieu; Louis Armstrong was there, and so were Bessie Smith, Ethel Waters, and the piano virtuoso Fats Waller. This last one famously responded to a white woman's request for a "definition" of jazz by saying, "Lady, if you don't know, I can't tell you." Perhaps that lady was slumming and never did "get it"; nonetheless, the Harlem jazz clubs reinvigorated the musical culture of America.

The idea of the New Negro was much in the air. This term, coined by Alain Locke, signified someone who was committed to erasing the stereotypes and destroying the obstacles that were placed in the way of black achievement. Du Bois was concerned that blacks be accepted as individuals and not stereotyped.

From his pulpit at *The Crisis,* Du Bois promoted the careers of Marian Anderson, Paul Robeson, Claude McKay, Langston Hughes, and other black artists. When black or white writers portrayed blacks in ways that he thought demeaned the race as a whole, he struck back, objecting to Van Vechten's *Nigger Heaven* and McKay's *Back to Harlem* as perpetuating the image of black men as sensualists.

Claude McKay (1889–1948)

One of the earliest and most central figures of the Harlem Renaissance was born in Jamaica. Claude McKay, born to peasant parents, was brought up on the poetry of Keats, Milton, and Shelley. He published two books in Kingston, Jamaica, before joining Booker T. Washington's Tuskeegee Institute and spending time at Kansas State College. Eventually, he moved to Greenwich Village, then as now a venue associated with leftist politics and artistic experimentation.

McKay was dismayed by the racism he encountered in America:

> Although she feeds me bread of bitterness,
> And sinks into my throat her tiger's tooth,
> Stealing my breath of life, I will confess
> I love this cultured hell that tests my youth!

His anger found concentrated expression in the two books of his that reached wide audiences, *Harlem Shadows* (1922) and *Home to Harlem* (1928), the first novel by a black writer to become a best-seller. His most famous poem, "If We Must Die," was inspired by the "Red Summer" of 1919, so called because of the bloodshed that occurred during race riots that followed World War I. Many black veterans who had fought in Woodrow Wilson's war to "preserve democracy" applied for jobs also sought by white workers in the North, leading to intense conflict and violence.

> Like men we'll face the murderous, cowardly pack,
> Pressed to the wall, dying, but fighting back!

After his first two books, McKay used mostly traditional forms. If this structure feels imposed, rather than naturally accommodated to the writing, and the language too direct, McKay was working for a cause, and that cause, as Alain Locke suggested, was paramount. The Marxism-Communism to which McKay was attracted is doubtless behind the poem, but no reader of it would see a program in this or in McKay's other sonnets and formal, rather antiquated verse: "The White City," "Dawn in New York," "Harlem Shadows" or "Jasmines."

It is a different case with his novel *Home to Harlem.* Although W. E. B. Du Bois criticized the novel for perpetuating black stereotypes, *Home to Harlem* is still an authoritative performance.

McKay's Marxism is not integrated into the plots of his books. The characters discuss Marxist ideas and sometimes wish that "the indecent horde [could] get its chance at the privileged things of life," but the novels never reach the point of showing this state. By the time he wrote his last novel, McKay was living abroad and apart from the Harlem milieu where he had gained a fine reputation that slowly declined. He returned to the United States in 1934 and later converted to Roman Catholicism.

Jean Toomer (1894–1967): *Cane* (1923)

Jean Toomer, 28, from rural Georgia, wrote one book. It burst on the Harlem scene with grand success when it appeared in 1923 from the mainstream publisher Liveright. Toomer had come to the attention of writers and critics when his sketches, poems, and stories appeared in literary magazines of the 1920s, such as *The Double Dealer, Dial,* and *Little Review,* where many famous writers—Sherwood Anderson, Hemingway, even Joyce—first appeared. Waldo Frank, Allen Tate, as well as black critics (Lola Rodge, William Stanley Braithwaite) hailed *Cane* as the work of a soon-to-be-major writer. *Cane* is, in fact, a major book of the Harlem Renaissance. It was perfectly adapted to the times, a worthy complement to Sherwood Anderson's *Winesburg, Ohio* (1919) and Hemingway's *In Our Time* (1925) and, like them, experimental in form, deriving power from its sense of the life beneath the surface of daily existence. It tells its story through a variety of voices and persons as Toomer manipulates the distance between the reader and his story.

To create *Cane,* Toomer took the lyrical stories and poems he had been publishing and put them into an intuitively right sequence. There are three sections. The result is an impressionistic collection, unified by tone and place, that captures a moment in African American history. Interspersed with these short stories Toomer inserts lyric poems ("Conversion," "Portrait in Georgia") in the way Hemingway interleaves vignettes between the stories in *In Our Time.* With its concentration on a variety of voices and forms and its disconnections, both those within the stories and the collagelike assemblage of the book, *Cane* is the Harlem Renaissance's most distinctly modernist production.

Cane had an impact that could have been greater only if Toomer had continued to write. However, he had done what he wanted to do. His long silence was one in which his achievement reverberated but then faded as the century wore on. It returned when the book was rediscovered in the 1970s.

Countee Cullen (1903–1946)

Countee Cullen burst on the literary scene in 1925, the year his first and most important collection of poems, *Color,* appeared. Cullen was still an M. A. candidate at Harvard when the book appeared and won five prizes. His aim was not "propaganda" but pure poetry: "If I am going to be a poet at all, I am going to be a POET and not a NEGRO POET."

Color was praised by the established black writer James Weldon Johnson and, in effusive terms that must have given its author great satisfaction, by Alain Locke. "*Color* transcends all the limiting qualifications that might be brought forward if it were merely a work of talent . . . it is the work of a Negro poet writing for the most part out of the intimate emotional experience of race, but the adjective is for the first time made irrelevant, so thoroughly has he poeticized the substance and fused it with the universally human moods of life."

This is high praise indeed. However, without ever PROSELYTIZING, almost all of Cullen's memorable verse is on the subject of race. His most anthologized poem, which scholars of Harlem Renaissance maintain was known by heart by African Americans of the 1920s, is "Heritage."

> What is Africa to me:
> Copper sun or scarlet sea . . .

The poem is written in rhymed couplets. Its rhythm is a mesmerizing TROCHAIC TETRAMETER that recalls the "great drums throbbing through the air" and "the unremittant beat" mentioned in the poem—all unconscious reminders of the speaker's African roots. Set against these sensual images is the poet's alienation from a Christianity he has come to adopt but that for him is inevitably white: "wishing He I served were black." This poem—unlike Cullen's later "The Black Christ," written in the same meter but less mechanically imposed—concludes in irresolution. That lack of closure gives the poem a tension that keeps it alive for its readers.

Color was a promising debut. Some of its short poems have lodged in the public mind. No later book by Cullen reached the intensity of his initial effort.

Cullen was married, briefly, to W. E. B. Du Bois's daughter Yolande. He taught English and French at Frederick Douglass Junior High School in New York. One of his students was James Baldwin, who later became a distinguished novelist and essayist. A translator and sometime novelist, Cullen collected his poems in *On These I Stand,* one year before his death in 1946.

Langston Hughes (1902–1967)

The writer of the Harlem Renaissance who has risen to the greatest visibility in recent years is the poet, novelist, essayist, playwright, and librettist Langston Hughes. Born in Missouri, Hughes began to write in mid-adolescence, under the influence of the poetry of Walt Whitman, especially as Whitman was imitated by the midwestern American poet Carl Sandburg. A student at Columbia University in New York, he was in the midst of the excitement of the Harlem Renaissance and at nineteen published one of his best known poems in Du Bois's *The Crisis,* "The Negro Speaks of Rivers."

> I've known rivers:
> I've known rivers ancient as the world and older than
> the flow of human blood in human veins.

This poem, one of Hughes's best, boldly embraces the world. Its succinct embodiment and quiet statement use the free- verse techniques of its models and applies them to black culture.

Boldness was a hallmark of the early Hughes. His 1926 essay "The Negro Artist and the Racial Mountain" announces again the New Negro, able to stand on his own and indifferent to the opinions of whites or blacks. "We younger Negro artists . . . intend to express our individual dark-skinned selves without fear or shame. If white people are pleased, we are glad. If they are not, it doesn't matter. We know we are beautiful. And ugly too. The tom-tom cries and the tom-tom laughs. If colored people are pleased we are glad. If they are not, their displeasure doesn't matter either. We build our temples for tomorrow, strong as we know how, and we stand on top of the mountain, free within ourselves." This was a stance that even W. E. B. Du Bois could champion.

Hughes soon proved to be a magpie when it came to poetic technique, in that, like the magpie who steals objects to build its nest, Hughes readily absorbed whatever was around him. By the time he had completed his first collection of poetry, *Weary Blues* (1926), he had begun the poetic practice that would characterize his work: picking up rhythms from songs, especially African American blues and jazz, whether from the Harlem musicians of the 1920s or from Dizzy Gillespie and Charlie Parker. He wanted to be a poet of the people, and he used the diction of the common people and adapted their popular structures for his poetry. "Fire" (1927) mimics the evangelical rhythms of gospel preaching, half way between chant and song.

> Fire, Lord!
> Fire gonna burn ma soul!

Like McKay and Cullen, Hughes writes about black experience, and, like them, he expanded in the 1930s as his awareness of ideologies grew. "Scottsboro," about the famous Alabama trial where nine black youths were convicted on a trumped-up rape charge, identifies the defendants in the case with the rebellious slave Nat Turner, as well as with Moses and Joan of Arc. "White Man" asks, "Is your name spelled / C-A-P-I-T-A-L-I-S-T?"

In his enormous poetic output—more than 800 poems—Hughes managed, like Cullen, to compose a few lyrics that have stayed with readers, notably his first poem and "Harlem," which asks the famous question, "What happens to a dream deferred?" and answers it by asking in a chilling final line, "does it explode?" He is still beloved because he was a central figure in the Harlem Renaissance and because he opened up a technique of using musical rhythms that others (poet Michael Harper in the 1970s, for one) found useful. His 717 *Collected Poems* went through eleven printings in eight years after its initial appearance. Many poets seek a broad, diverse, and sympathetic audience. Langston Hughes got one.

Zora Neale Hurston (1891–1960)

Zora Neale Hurston, though from the South, is often associated with the Harlem Renaissance because, starting in 1925, she lived

**Countee Cullen, photograph taken
by Carl Van Vechten, 1941**
In city clothes even in this woodsy setting, Cullen
remained devoted to New York and Harlem.

in Harlem among its major figures. Early on she wrote stories, one of which prompted a request from a publisher and resulted in the publication of her first novel. Hurston was interested in black folklore. After her first novel, *Jonah's Gourd Vine* (1934), appeared she released a collection of folk tales, *Mules and Men* (1935). Hurston even tried to work one of her folk tales into a play in collaboration with Langston Hughes but without success.

Shortly afterward, Hurston wrote the novel acknowledged as her masterpiece, *Their Eyes Were Watching God* (1937). It is an extraordinary book, even more remarkable when contrasted with some of the politicized, angry social literature of the Harlem Renaissance, for *Their Eyes Were Watching God* has no overt element of protest. It is a story of love and self-realization. Although the narrative voice is in traditional English, the dialogue is in dialect. The novel is as funny as it is perceptive, a unique document in African American letters.

The time in which the events take place is probably the mid-1930s. Janie Crawford tells her life story to her best friend Phoeby Watson. Phoeby complains that Janie was too old to have married her husband Tea Cake. Janie explains how this marriage came about by explaining her two previous marriages.

Raised by her grandmother, Janie is innocent of the concept of race; she has no idea that she is black. When this identification is forced on her, she becomes a different person. Moreover, as the book makes clear, Janie was simply, naturally sexually awake. Bees and pollen stirred her. Seeing this, her nanny unfortunately forces her to marry. It is an African American story of the fall.

The novel recounts the end of this marriage and a second, this time to a man named Joe, who also turns out to be unsuitable for Janie. She needs spiritual nourishment.

Food, in fact, literal and spiritual, is an important continuing metaphor in the novel. Janie needs to be fed as well as to feed. Eventually, into Janie's life walks a man whose name refers to food—Janie's third husband to be, Tea Cake. After some time and some doubting, Janie sells a store she has been operating to live with Tea Cake in the Florida Everglades, in the "muck." "Folks don't do nothin' down dere but make money and fun and foolishness."

Its affirmation of self-sufficient African American life and the self-realization and fulfillment of the main character give *Their Eyes Were Watching God* the same tensile, undemanding strength as Sarah Orne Jewett's *Country of the Pointed Firs*. Without raising the decibel level of the prose, or indulging in modernist TROPES, but relying on her own blend of folklore and understanding, Zora Neale

■ ■ ■ ■ STEREOTYPICAL WHITES ■ ■ ■ ■

W. E. B. Du Bois's sense of cliché was penetrating. His comical 1922 satirical SQUIB "Ten Phrases" shows the white mentality that Du Bois was fighting.

The following ten phrases are recommended to white students in Southern colleges as quite sufficient for all possible discussion of the race problem:

1. The Southerner is the Negro's Best Friend.
2. Slavery was Beneficial to the Negro.
3. The Races will Never Mix.
4. All Negro Leaders are Mulattos.
5. The Place for the Negro is in the South.
6. I love my Black Mammy.
7. Do you want your sister to marry a Nigger?
8. Do not disturb the present friendly relations between the races.
9. The Negro must be kept in his place.
10. Lynching is the defense of Southern womanhood.

Du Bois' method of combating this racist mindset is especially effective because of his straight-faced humor. Instead of explaining what is wrong with each of these statements, he lets them stand by themselves, so that the utterer is convicted by his own racism. Such stupidity, Du Bois is claiming, is its own best commentary. This posture is aristocratic, superior without being condescending, and unanswerable.

Hurston wrote a novel beside which the more strident and insistently melodramatic books of other African American novelists may seem contrived.

Two novels, *Moses, Man of the Mountain* (1939) and *Seraph on the Suwannee* (1948), followed, as did legal and financial troubles. In 1946 Hurston returned to New York but found she could not live there because of the racism and exclusion she experienced there. The locus of the Great Migration had become "a basement to hell." She moved back to Florida. Although she continued to write profiles and essays for magazines, her submissions were increasingly rejected. Health problems plagued her. She died in obscurity in 1960, her writing forgotten, but in 1995 her work, including previous uncollected short stories, was collected in the Library of America series.

Carl Van Vechten (1880–1964)

All the writers thus far in this chapter—Alain Locke, W. E. B. Du Bois, Jean Toomer, Claude McKay, Countee Cullen, Langston Hughes, and Zora Neale Hurston—were African American. Carl Van Vechten was white, but he belongs in the Harlem Renaissance because of his support and understanding of African American writers and because of one of his novels, *Nigger Heaven* (1926).

Van Vechten's wide-ranging interests led him naturally to Harlem and African-American artists with whose marginal position in American culture he felt an instinctive sympathy and whom personally he came to like. James Weldon Johnson, author of a classic novel, *The Autobiography of an Ex-Colored Man,* was a close friend, as was W. E. B. Du Bois. Through them and through his position as a novelist, party-goer, and party-giver extraordinaire—his daybook *The Splendid Drunken Twenties,* published in 2003, records a whirlwind of socializing—he came to know Langston Hughes, Paul Robeson, Duke Ellington, Claude McKay, Zora Neale Hurston, and later James Baldwin.

Although he wrote seven novels, Van Vechten today is remembered for *Nigger Heaven,* which sold an astonishing 500,000 copies in its day. The book presents low life in Harlem as a model of PRIMITIVISM: "Hottentots and Bantus swaying under the amber moon. Love, sex, passion . . . hate." However, *Nigger Heaven* is also a survey of all levels of black

▪ ▪ THE TRIAL OF ▪ ▪ THE SCOTTSBORO BOYS

In 1931 nine black youths, riding the rails, fought a number of whites—two of whom were women—also riding the rails. The blacks pushed the whites off the train. When one of the whites went to the police, the order was given "to round up every Negro on the train and bring them to Scottsboro."

The trial rapidly became a brawl of racism and wild accusation. The white women, fearing vagrancy charges, claimed they had been gang raped. They were made into pillars of southern womanhood. One even claimed that one of the blacks had chewed off one of her breasts.

A rapid trial occurred in which the prosecutor declared "Guilty or not, let's get rid of these niggers." The verdict was guilty, despite the evidence that while both women had had sex, it had been neither recent nor forced. The case was appealed and became a CAUSE CÉLÈBRE. Albert Einstein and Theodore Dreiser protested for the blacks. Represented by a "New York Jew nigger lover" lawyer, as attorney Samuel Leibowitz was called, the defendants saw their case thrown out by the Supreme Court in 1932. It wasn't until 1977, long after many of the original Scottsboro boys had died, that the remaining defendant, Clarence Norris, was pardoned and given $10,000 compensation for the injustices he had suffered.

■ ■ ■ ■ "Branches Without Roots" ■ ■ ■ ■
(—Their Eyes Were Watching God)

Zora Neale Hurston died in obscurity in 1960. Her grave was unmarked until 1973, when the African American writer Alice Walker, who considered *Their Eyes Were Watching God* a key book in her experience ("There is no book more important to me than this one"), pretending to be the niece of Hurston, traveled to Fort Pierce, found what information she could, and located Hurston's burial place in an obscure cemetery. In the Garden of Heavenly Rest, Walker had a tomb-stone erected, reading

Zora Neale Hurston
A Genius of the South
1901–1960
Novelist Folklorist Anthropologist

The grave itself sits near the wild, scraggly Florida landscape vividly depicted in Hurston's novel—not perhaps as prominent a venue as the importance of the book warrants but in other ways entirely appropriate.

Through Walker's efforts Hurston has rightfully reclaimed her position in American letters. *Their Eyes Were Watching God* is often taught in the classroom, and the entire work of a once-forgotten American author has now appeared in two volumes in The Library of America series, the set of books of canonical American literature, writing of permanent national interest. Hurston now stands on the shelf with Twain, James, Douglass, and Melville.

society. A sensitive black intelligentsia is most hurt by racial prejudice, the novel suggests, while wealthy blacks are far removed from white prejudice because of their money. Indeed, white guests are flattered to be invited to wealthy black homes.

Van Vechten devoted the last 32 years of his life to photography, and it is thanks to him that the Beinecke Museum at Yale University in New Haven, Connecticut, and the Library of Congress in Washington, D. C., have memorable images of many black writers and artists, as well as of W. H. Auden, F. Scott Fitzgerald, William Faulkner, Thomas Mann, Eugene O'Neill, and many important cultural figures of the Jazz Age and the twentieth century.

5. Modernism in Poetry and Drama

The impulse to experiment was not confined to prose, and modernism affected poetry in ways less immediate than the imitators of Eliot and Pound (Gertrude Stein was inimitable). If modernism means experimentation in the arts, there was considerable borrowing of techniques from one art by another, and some of this cross-pollination gave new vitality to poetry and drama. In particular painting and the techniques of European artists affected the way writers conceived of their work and executed it.

Surrealism and Expressionism

One of the painters closely associated with modernist movements was Salvador Dalí (1904–1989), from Catalonia in Spain. Dalí was especially influenced by Freud's concept of the subconscious. His paintings were not literal depictions of the known world but disconcerting "realistic" representations of the subconscious. Objects, such as watches in his famous *The Persistence of Memory* (1931), acquire properties that they do not ordinarily possess; for example, they melt. Odd and disembodied forms occur; they appear as though they are human flesh, but they may be distorted. They often evoke breasts, genitals, and buttocks, and they are usually set in vacant, empty landscapes of no charm or allure.

Dalí's emphasis on sexuality, especially perverse and disturbing varieties of sex, originates from Freud's *The Interpretation of Dreams* (1900). In that book the Viennese psychiatrist argued that dreams, originating in the subconscious, deal symbolically with conflicts profoundly disturbing to the dreamer, in order to keep the dreamer asleep. As the rational mind gives way to the subconscious, upsetting notions rise, transformed, to the surface. These notions spring from two psychic domains, sex and death, EROS and THANATOS. Freud believed that both males and females harbor variously directed sexual impulses—toward their parents, toward other family members, or toward friends, who are perceived as projections of mothers and fathers. However, at the same time as the emotional makeup or psyche of a person is directed toward reproduction or perpetuation (sex, the erotic drive), it is paradoxically directed toward death, toward the cessation of all conflict.

Dalí's dreamlike pictures, influenced by Freud's writings, emanate from Freud's model. Disembodied sexual parts abound in a setting whose emptiness is the absence of all life, the wish for death itself. Time, a human construct, imprisons; no one escapes. Dalí's art is, perhaps, the most intense example of SURREALISM—a term coined by the French surrealist André Breton in 1924.

Literature also readily adopted Freud's ideas of the subconscious. Sometimes, especially in poetry and more readily in fiction, literature was surreal. In the theater, however, representation of the unconscious took another form. Because plays are staged in actual space and time with real actors in them, the fanciful nature of the unconscious is difficult to represent. Surreal plays, such as those of the American humorist Ring Lardner, are rare. Instead, the theater came to use symbols and stage devices to objectify an inner reality. The plays of Eugene O'Neill, for instance, written under the sway of Freud, are instead examples of EXPRESSIONISM. They use symbols perceptible to the audience to suggest the inner life of the characters before them.

Although some poetry—especially French and German—committed itself to surrealism and used images drawn from Freudian psychology, American poetry resisted the tendency. Some poets, such as Robert Frost, by temperament or by conscious choice, avoided these trends altogether, whereas others, such as William Carlos Williams, adhered to the imagism developed by Ezra Pound in the mid-nineteen teens. At least one great poet, Wallace Stevens, developed a world of imagination independent of cultural movements, however accidentally evocative of them the work might appear.

Robert Frost (1874–1963)

Robert Frost, though contemporary with all these trends, was deliberately antimodernist, his poetic skill acting as a brake on the impulses of modernism. He showed what could be done supremely well in traditional forms. Skeptical and reserved, Frost, even more than Langston Hughes or Hughes's model Carl Sandburg (1878–1967), became a revered public personality. Behind Frost's public persona, however, lay a calculating, difficult, highly intelligent, sometimes generous, sometimes selfish, manipulative man, clever, shrewd, and complex. His air suggested that he was a simple rustic, a fellow who liked nature walks. Reading the poetry dispels this image and replaces it with one wilier and more hard nosed.

Frost read the modernists but never felt he had to be one of them. Early and late Frost is skeptical, reserved, ironic, dubious, and playful. Perhaps Frost's humorously unhelpful notes to the original 1947 edition of his collection *Steeple Bush* were a parody of Eliot's notes to *The Waste Land*. With Frost one never knows.

Frost's first books, *A Boy's Will* (1913) and *North of Boston* (1914), were published in England, where Ezra Pound championed them and helped secure their publication. Although Frost and Pound maintained a guarded friendship—every relationship with Frost was guarded—the two men were not emotionally or temperamentally alike. If Pound on the page rants and screams, Frost maintains a steady iambic gait that breaks at key moments.

"Anything more than the truth would have seemed too weak," writes Frost in an early sonnet. If the modernists think the truth can be wrested only from new forms, Frost thinks that it is there if one listens and does not embellish. Why seek new forms when there may be nothing really new to say and the truth is all around us? "The fact is the sweetest dream that labor knows."

Frost's early poems fall into two categories: tightly organized lyrics, such as "Mowing," "After Apple Picking," "To Earthward," "Stopping By Woods on a Snowy Evening," and "Birches," whose suggestiveness and natural lyricism frequently conceal destructive and self-destructive impulses; and dramatic monologues of subtle ruthlessness, such as "The Death of the Hired Man," "A Servant to Servants," or "Home Burial," as harrowing an account of a family argument as was ever written. If a gap exists between a man and a woman, the poem says, it cannot be breached.

Unlike T. S. Eliot or William Carlos Williams, Robert Frost never wrote the big poem, the one that marks a watershed in his work or for his time. His own aims, as he declared them, were perhaps small: to write a few poems that would be "hard to get rid of." He certainly succeeded. Can any poet do more? Was that really all Frost hoped for? It sounds a shade defensive and overly modest. With Frost one never knows.

William Carlos Williams (1883–1963)

Although T. S. Eliot worked as a banker and later as an executive for an English publishing house and although other writers associated with modernism had jobs in order to support themselves, only William Carlos Williams and Wallace Stevens were serious practitioners in other fields. Williams was a pediatrician. Born in Rutherford, New Jersey, he attended medical school at the University of Pennsylvania, where he met Ezra Pound and his companion at that time, the poet H. D. (Hilda Doolittle). At first a strict disciple of imagism, Williams all his life was attracted to the "thingness" of poetry, its irreducible physicality, the permanence of the

Robert Frost photographed by Arthur Tourtillot
The portrait was made at the Bread Loaf Writer's Conference in Vermont, near Middlebury College, in 1925. Frost helped found the conference, reasoning that after Middlebury's School of English had finished, the two sweetest weeks of the Vermont summer were still to come. Bread Loaf is the oldest writer's conference in the country; Frost participated every year until his death in January 1963.

▪ ▪ ▪ ▪ FROST AND STEVENS ON POETRY ▪ ▪ ▪ ▪

No better way exists to highlight the different personalities of Robert Frost and Wallace Stevens than to place side by side their statements about poetry.

First Frost:

Poetry is what gets lost in translation.
Writing free verse is like playing tennis with the net down.
The chief reason for going to school is to get the impression that there is a book side to everything.
Like a piece of ice on a hot stove the poem must ride on its own meaning.
The practice of an art is more salutary than talk about it. There is nothing more composing than composition.

Then Wallace Stevens:

Money is a kind of poetry.
Authors are actors, books are theaters.
The eye sees less than the tongue says. The tongue says less than the mind thinks.
Poetry is the expression of the experience of poetry.
It is necessary to propose an enigma to the mind. The mind always proposes a solution.

---

image, which in Williams's and the imagists' views outlast any construction that may be put on it.

At one point Williams called his poetics "objectivism," a paring away of a poem to its essence, its core. He did not want emotion to enter into the poem directly. That was the space for the reader.

As Williams continued this practice he underplayed himself as an artist, so that a reader coming on his famous eight-line poem from *Spring and All* (1923) that begins

    so much depends
    upon

may miss the joke in "depends." The word literally means to hang from, and the next line does hang. However, it consists of the word "upon," whose suspension is ironic. That suspension thereby suggests the importance of the red wheelbarrow itself, to which we are then introduced. By separating "wheel" "barrow" and "rain" "water," Williams breaks these names into their component parts, underscoring the "thingness" of them. The poem has the simplicity of a stripped and modernist painting, an image set forth in primitive and spare loveliness.

It has another characteristic, as well, that Williams was to exploit throughout the rest of his career. More than simply using VERNACULAR, Williams wants to capture the rhythms of American speech. The great modernists who preceded him, his friend Ezra Pound and T. S. Eliot, centered themselves in foreign cultures. They lived in Europe. Williams, however, was insistently American. He remained in Rutherford, New Jersey. Unlike Eliot and Pound, who include foreign languages (in the case of Pound they include translations from one foreign language into a second that the poem then renders into English), Williams writes in American.

"So much depends," begin these eight lines, as though the whole is an offhand exercise, a casually tossed away comment, without any elaborate explanation, retrieved by Williams and presented to the reader as something found by accident. The two beat second lines ("upon," "barrow") suggest that the speaker is thinking this out as he is speaking.

It is impossible to imagine an English poet writing in just this way.

■ ■ *PATERSON* ■ ■

The poetical impulse of Williams sustained itself into old age. For the last fifteen years of his life, he was occupied with an epic-length poem, *Paterson*, published in five separate volumes. The hero of the book is the city in New Jersey of that name. It is at once personal and public. Rutherford, where Williams lived and practiced pediatrics, is near Paterson, and Williams relished its energy and spoiled beauty. He describes Paterson with the energetic fervor of a lover. The book follows the Passaic River through the city, interlarding the ecstasy with prose letters and descriptions—a catalog meant to encapsulate American experience in the twentieth century as a Whitmanesque answer to Eliot's *Waste Land*.

Paterson has been variously judged by critics, but all have responded to the grandeur of its conception and its gusto. The first book, "The Delineaments of the Giants," contains Williams's famous dictum "no ideas but in things" and describes the Passaic River as it descends on the city

> and crashes from the edge of
> the gorge
> in a recoil of spray and rain-
> bow mists—

The weight of tradition, in many respects an advantage for an English writer by providing a set of ready-made tools to use, or, as the case may be, to rebel against, has the disadvantage of bookishness. It urges the writer to produce literature that comes out of other literature. Williams, in taking literature from the common

■ ■ ■ ■ Snobbery and the General Reader ■ ■ ■ ■

American publishing in the nineteenth and twentieth centuries was centered in Boston and then New York. Some snobbism attaches to these cities. At a dinner at Holy Cross in 1910, one John Collins Brossidy famously said

And this is good old Boston,
The home of the bean and the cod,
Where the Lowells talk only to Cabots,
And the Cabots talk only to God.

In the second instance, one might think of Saul Steinberg's cartoon in *The New Yorker* magazine in which the map of America is viewed from the perspective of a New Yorker, with states increasingly distant receiving progressively smaller amounts of space.

Such snobbery was completely foreign to William Carlos Williams and to many others. Middle-class Americans to a certain extent disdained or were not interested in the writing of the modernists. Few of their books appeared on the bestseller lists. However, William Carlos Williams's poetry, which uses the concepts of imagism and modernism, was never on those lists either, and his democratic, egalitarian sensibility reached a relatively elite audience. The middle class was, however, comfortable with biography. Hemingway, Faulkner, and Joyce were all on the cover of *Time* magazine in the 1930s and became known to thousands of Americans who never read their books. Culture absorbs and embraces new perspectives slowly.

speech of Americans, revitalizes the process of writing, in the same democratic spirit as Walt Whitman (1819–1892), whose *Leaves of Grass* (1847–1892) is written in a free verse that is meant to suggest simplicity and directness. (Whitman's poetry is neither simple nor as direct as it at first seems, of course.)

Many of the followers of Williams—who, like Hemingway, was extremely influential—have adopted his manner without the depth of his art. Nor can they capture the supreme lyricism of his late work, as notably displayed in "Asphodel, That Greeny Flower."

Wallace Stevens (1879–1955)

It would be difficult to imagine two poets more different than William Carlos Williams and Wallace Stevens. If Williams deliberately uses

American language, Stevens adopts a language that, while mostly American, is anything but the speech of ordinary people. The titles of some poems in Stevens's first book and the title itself, point to the fanciful, the gaudy, the elaborate: "Fabliau of Florida," "Homunculus et La Belle Étoile," "The Comedian as the Letter C," "The Apostrophe to Vincentine," "Jasmine's Beautiful Thoughts Underneath the Willow," and "Peter Quince at the Clavier." Plainly these poems come from a universe of precious objects, with language to match. Although Stevens is a modern and a very different kind of poet from his contemporaries, a modernist like Eliot or Pound he is not, yet his poems could have been written only in an atmosphere liberated by the modernists.

Stevens, like Williams, had a nonacademic job. A vice president of the Hartford Insurance Company, he split his time between literature and business. Although the indefatigable and ubiquitous Carl Van Vechten recommended his first collection, *Harmonium,* to Alfred A. Knopf for publication and although by the end of his life Stevens had met Ernest Hemingway (with whom he, drunkenly, tried to box), Robert Frost, and Marianne Moore, Stevens's work was done apart from literary circles. Living in Hartford, Connecticut, with occasional vacations elsewhere, Stevens pursued his own world of the imagination; a reader would never suspect that Stevens was an insurance man; his colleagues in Hartford remained unaware of his writing. If his poems have unexpected connections and seem at times surreal, that has nothing to do with a system or set of beliefs or an identification with any "movement." As he wrote once to a critic, "We are dealing with poetry, not philosophy."

It is poetry of a singularly pure sort, devoted to the imagination, which, whatever its sources, is sufficient unto itself. In "Disillusionment of Ten O'Clock" an "old sailor" "catches tigers / in red weather."

Still other poems of Wallace Stevens have other emphases and offer verbal pyrotechnics beyond those in *Harmonium.* Unlike T. S. Eliot, whose personal experiences provided the impetus for his poems, Wallace Stevens needed only for his mind to function, for it was fed by the interplay of sound and idea, with the one suggesting the other, and the other always suggesting another one.

Realism and Modernism in the Theater

Given the practical difficulties, a surreal play might be challenging or impossible to stage. Surrealism, as practiced by Salvador Dalí, is not unknown to the theater, although productions have been rare. In America, the one writer of surreal plays was the humorist Ring Lardner (1885–1933). Long before the absurdist, experimental plays of the French surrealist André Breton (1896–1966) and the Irish-French playwright Samuel Beckett (1906–1989), Lardner produced nine whimsical, wildly hysterical short plays, one of which, *The Tridget of Greva* (the title gives no information), was produced in a revue. Although not among Lardner's best-known works—his short stories and the epistolary sports novel *You Know Me Al*—they have a following of their own. To the right sensibility they break experience down into helpless mirth—engendering nonsense. Robert Frost laughed himself silly over *I Gaspiri, The Upholsterers.* J. D. Salinger, through Holden Caulfield, as well as the American critic Maxwell Geismar both admire Lardner's plays.

Lardner, possibly without quite realizing it, happened on avant-garde theater. The dialogue, full of nonsequiturs and deliberately bad puns and misunderstandings gives the reader (or viewer) an eerie sense of regression, something like formal nonsense without the logic or rigor nonsense writing requires.

> ■ ■ **SURREAL THEATER:** ■ ■
> **RING LARDNER**
>
> One of the surprising aspects of Lardner's surreal plays—if anything in such a context can be said to surprise more than anything else—is that the stage directions and casts of characters are as entertaining and strange as the dialogue and action. The cast of *I Gaspiri, The Upholsterers*, for instance includes the following.
>
> Padre, a Priest.
> Sethso ⎫
> Gethso ⎭ Both Twins
> Wayshattan, a Shepherd's Boy
> Two Capitalists.*
> Wama Tammisch, her daughter.
> Klema, a Janitor's third daughter.
> Kevela, their mother, afterwards their aunt.
>
> *NOTE: The two Capitalists don't appear in this show.
>
> Not only do the two capitalists not appear but also the play has nothing to do with upholstering or anything like it. We are living in a random world that makes no effort at sense.
>
>

FIRST STRANGER	Where was you born?
SECOND STRANGER	Out of wedlock.
FIRST STRANGER	That's a mighty pretty country around there.

In at least one of these short plays, *Quadroon,* Lardner mocked the preeminent dramatist of his time, the one indisputable expressionistic playwright of distinction America produced, Eugene O'Neill.

Eugene O'Neill (1888–1953)

Eugene O'Neill's father was a New York theatrical producer, and although O'Neill spent some of his early years in the company of actors and producers, he also led a nomadic existence for the first two decades of his life. He shipped to Honduras, Argentina, and South Africa in search of work and experience, eventually returning to the theater in Connecticut and afterward, productively, in Provincetown, Massachusetts, then as now a MECCA for artistic experimentation.

O'Neill's interest in theater was well timed. Although motion picture theaters had existed for more than a decade by the time O'Neill began writing, the films were all silent. The theater was still the best forum for public performance of a serious nature.

Beyond the Horizon (1920) and *Anna Christie* (1920) were the first two plays that followed O'Neill's apprenticeship in Provincetown. Both of these plays won Pulitzer Prizes.

In *Anna Christie*, the sordid family life, the pessimistic view of human nature, and the inescapability of character reflect O'Neill's deep reading in Greek tragedies and his willingness to portray low life in grimly naturalistic terms. The experiences of the characters, especially the heroine's, determine their fate. *Anna Christie* has no moral in tow, no uplifting message or promise of redemption. Such is what we refer to as naturalism.

The same year as *Anna Christie* came O'Neill's first major exercise in expressionism, *The Emperor Jones.* The hero of the title is Brutus Jones, a "tall, powerfully-built, full-blooded negro of middle age." Although "his eyes are alive with a deep, cunning intelligence," "yet there is something ridiculous about his grandeur." Jones rules an island in the West Indies. Cruel and manipulative, he has become rich fooling "dese black trash." However, he has a plan to escape from his island when the exploited begin to rebel. As he boasts to the cockney trader Henry Smithers, he will flee to France and nothing can stop him except a silver bullet.

As soon as he offers this explanation, he hears the beat of a drum. Smithers explains: "The blacks is 'oldin' a bloody meetin', 'avin a war dance, gettin' their courage worked up b'fore they starts after you." The dialect gives a primitive feel to the play, an effect O'Neill enhances by staging the play almost entirely in darkness,

▪ ▪ ▪ ▪ THE THEATER IN O'NEILL'S AMERICA ▪ ▪ ▪ ▪

America had its share of theatrical companies, both in New York, the center of drama, and elsewhere when O'Neill was starting to write, but it had had no world-class dramatist until O'Neill. Instead American theaters offered a number of experiences, not all of which were pure drama, such as the circus, burlesque, vaudeville, rodeos, and medicine shows. Most of the smaller, non-New York theaters offered a variety of different stage entertainments in addition to straight plays, although there were exceptions, and the theater in Provincetown, Massachusetts, with which O'Neill associated himself, was one of the best in the country.

This situation had both advantages and disadvantages. Theater was certainly enriched by contact with other genres. W. C. Fields's (1880–1946) clowning, for example, owed much to vaudeville and juggling acts. However, there were encroachments and the situation was in flux. Just at the time O'Neill began his career, new competitors to theater appeared. The first motion picture was made in 1903, and by 1920 the nickel cinema was commonplace. And by the mid-1920s the radio craze was sweeping throughout America.

Films in the 1920s were silent. Not until 1929 was the first widely distributed sound film created. O'Neill's plays in the 1920s thus offered things that movies could not: extended dialogue interwoven with theatrical affects. The playwright had at his command a precious gift not yet available to directors and producers of films—language—as well as another resource not available to the radio programmer: a visual stage. A master at conceiving stage affects and a penetrating writer, O'Neill may be the last complete man of live theater.

where fears can most easily dominate, and also through a simple expressionistic device.

> From the distant hills comes the faint, steady thump of a tom-tom, low and vibrating. It starts at a rate exactly corresponding to normal pulse beat—72 to the minute—and continues at a gradually accelerating rate from this point uninterruptedly to the very end of the play.

The Emperor Jones expresses Jones's elemental character; the faster, progressively louder tom-tom both unnerves Jones and aligns

**Eugene O'Neill, one of the most photogenic
writers who ever lived**
O'Neill is shown here in 1933 with his third wife, Carlotta Monterey O'Neill.
Although their relationship was marked by quarrels and bitterness, they loved
each other deeply. He was married to Carlotta when he died in 1953.

■ ■ ■ ■ Eugene O'Neill, Alcoholism, and Writing ■ ■ ■ ■
Eugene O'Neill's unhappy experiences with alcoholism and the centrality of liquor and addictions in his plays raise the general question of why so many American writers were alcoholics. Of the writers in this volume, Faulkner, Fitzgerald, Hemingway, Lardner, Lewis, Steinbeck, and O'Neill would all be so classified.

It is easy to see which writers drank to excess, but it is harder to understand why they drank. Prohibition may explain the social attractiveness of drinking for Fitzgerald and his peers, but it does not explain the profound and tenacious attractiveness alcohol had for them or why even when they tried to stop drinking they could not.

Part of an answer might be found in *The Iceman Cometh*. The bar flies are devoted to their "pipe dreams" in order to keep going; dull reality makes life unbearable. Even though the metaphor of pipe dreams comes from drug taking—opium pipe dreams—the motivation to escape from ordinary life is similar. Moreover, after a while, as the Tyrone family in *Long Day's Journey into Night* discovers, the problems compound themselves. As Fitzgerald wrote once, "I couldn't get sober enough to be able to tolerate being sober."

Of course, not all people who find reality disagreeable become alcoholics, and no one has yet come up with a satisfactory explanation for the high incidence of alcoholism among literary figures. As Donald W. Goodwin, a doctor who has studied this problem, writes, "The origin of alcoholism is as inscrutable as the mystery of . . . writing talent."

the audience, whose pulses, presumably by sympathetic vibration, have quickened into fury, with Jones's anguish. *The Emperor Jones* induces feelings with elemental directness, rather than by words or argument. At its heart, expressionism is not intellectual. It is instinctive and MIMETIC however much it may owe to psychology.

O'Neill continued to explore the possibilities of theatrical expression. Although the naturalism was matched with a classic tragedy in his New England drama *Desire Under the Elms* (1924), the play in which expressionistic devices, psychology, and Greek fate are aligned with stream of consciousness is another with a New England setting, *Strange Interlude* (1927).

Set in the part of America most associated with Puritanism and stifled desires, *Strange Interlude* recounts the frustrations of Nina

Leeds, daughter of a possessive university professor, in terms that derive straight from Sigmund Freud. She tells her last husband that people are ruled by the impulse to die. "Our lives are merely strange dark interludes in the electrical display of God the father."

The Electra complex—Freud's formulation for the way in which females chose husbands who are like their fathers—hangs over this play. The subconscious is always evident as O'Neill shows the split between what people do and say and what their lonely, interior selves tell them. Thus, stream-of-consciousness techniques emerge in *Strange Interlude.* At one point Nina, at the same time as she is talking to her new husband Charles Marsden, alternately speaks, in her head, to her father, who started all her problems. The audience has to sort out this disturbing scene as best it can. In a further Freudian fusing of expressionism and psychology, Marsden replies, speaking to Nina, according to O'Neill's stage directions, "paternally—in her father's tone."

The source for these bitter family tragedies was O'Neill's own family life. His 1941 masterpiece *Long Day's Journey into Night* comes straight from his own background. There are four members of the Tyrone family: Mary, the drug addicted mother; James, a former stage idol clearly based on O'Neill's father James; and their two sons, Jamie and Edmund, the one an embittered drunk at 33 and the other an ill intellectual whose deepest impulses are suicidal. Each of the men throughout the course of the play tries to dominate the others with their understanding of what has happened, but it is the mother, as she slips into unreality, who has the last word. When Mary appears in her wedding gown, trying to recreate a time when she believed she was happy, the family realizes its own end is imminent. O'Neill's sense of time is Faulknerian: "The past is the present, isn't it?" asks Mary Tyrone. And she adds, "It's the future too."

O'Neill spread his personality throughout all of these characters yet at the same time kept true to his own memories. The closeness of the play to his life prevented O'Neill from giving it to the public when he wrote it. It was not produced on stage until three years after his death.

By his innovations of theatrical technique, his marrying of classical theater to modernist techniques, and the empathetic presentation of his doomed, ruined characters in all their pathetic yearnings and defeats, O'Neill dominated American theater for the first half of the twentieth century. His view is tragic. Understanding comes too late and is ineffective when it arrives. This is the truth that play after play of Eugene O'Neill reenacts.

6. Literary Culture of the Moderns

Modernism did not die. It was supplanted and reemerged in altered form in the 1980s. However, for a time it was buried. The events of history overtook it. Perhaps the most universal alteration of circumstances was the economic crisis of the 1930s, the GREAT DEPRESSION.

The causes of the Depression were many and mutually reinforcing. The one that casual students of history cite is the crash of the stock market, and that certainly contributed to the Depression, although by itself, it may not have caused it.

When people sell their stocks because of falling dividends or in anticipation of falling dividends or because conditions are so bad they can raise money no other way, the price is likely to drop. If enough stockholders sell, the stock may become worthless: No one will want it. If this happens often enough, as it did in 1929, the market as a whole crashes.

The crash had multiple consequences. Banks that had invested in the market were out of funds. People who put their savings in banks lost their money and had none to buy food and goods. Farmers who provided food and manufacturers of consumer goods had less of a market. Layoffs resulted. One failure reinforced another, and it seemed to many as though the entire economic system was not simply badly managed but wrong. The people most hurt were not rich investors, who still had resources, but ordinary working men and women. The distance between these groups was huge. John D. Rockefeller (1839–1937) was worth many millions of dollars and handed out dimes as charity.

Intellectuals who studied this situation believed that the cause was the pyramid of labor. Many at the bottom labored for a few at the top. In *Das Kapital* (1867), the German social and economic philosopher Karl Marx (1818–1883) condemned a system designed to produce money or capital that depended on selling goods for more than they were worth in terms of material workmanship: capitalism. It promoted inequalities and ultimately, Marx believed, was destined to self-destruct.

These ideas had great force in the 1930s when evidence of inequality was so immediate and when no solutions seemed at hand. The result was a surge in popularity of Marx's ideas—not only in his sharp criticism of the capitalist system but also in his (and others') vision of a system that could replace it and be fairer to all: COMMUNISM. Communism derives from the word "common." Its essential tenet is that all people own all property and share in the means of exploiting that property. The result is a classless system in which no one is better off than anyone else. Conflicts are minimized.

Communism is at odds with Freudianism, which situates conflict within the family structure. However, a Marxist would contend that the family structure—a mother and a father, each with different assigned and agreed-on tasks—is socially constructed, that is, not biological or natural but, rather, determined by social conditions. As a consequence, the theory suggested, family structure could be altered and would be altered over time as communism replaced capitalism. Whether that could ever take place is unclear. The most famous country to try to put Marx's ideas into practice, the Soviet Union, never did succeed in instituting true communism and collapsed. Human nature and history intervened.

The Soviet Union, however, was a country to which many artists and intellectuals were attracted in the 1930s. Older socialist writers, such as Theodore Dreiser, visited and variously approved of what they saw. Hemingway flirted with communist thinking in the 1930s. Fitzgerald saw himself as "essentially" communist. W. E. B. Du Bois, Countee Cullen, and Claude McKay wrote books that leaned toward communist thought because African Americans, disenfranchised or denied their rights under the old America, could see with special clarity the advantages of a classless society, where the color of their skin would not be an issue. Even popular writers, such as the detective novelist Dashiell Hammett (1894–1961), author of *Red Harvest* (1929), *The Maltese Falcon* (1930), *The Glass Key* (1931), and *The Thin Man* (1934), became "reds." The iconoclasm, the desperate partying of the 1920s, was over.

The most effective American literary artist whose works imply the need for Communism was John Steinbeck.

John Steinbeck (1902–1968)

Like William Faulkner, John Steinbeck took some time to discover the subject he was best able to treat in fiction, and, like Faulkner, he frequently made forays into other topics. He was born in Salinas, a modest town in the middle of one of California's great farming areas. Like other writers associated with the West—for example, Frank Norris (1870–1902)—Steinbeck has an openness, an uncomplicated willingness to accept simple people as they are. He came after a decade in which literary experimentation was dominant, where sheer artistry was a prime value in and of itself—the decade of Stein, Hemingway, Faulkner, and Fitzgerald, all stylists. Steinbeck pulled back from modernism, not because he wanted to rebel against it, but because his own experiences at a variety of jobs and his immediate sympathies were not oriented in that direction.

His third novel, *Tortilla Flat* (1935), captured the imagination of the public. Set near Monterey, California, it has no political message. It is a rambunctious, humorous, PICARESQUE story of peasants, drinking parties, love affairs, hardships, and simple persistence in a life that binds the characters into a community.

The novel that followed the agreeable comedy of *Tortilla Flat, In Dubious Battle* (1936), is a contrast. In place of gaily living peasants are earnest people who must work to make a living. There are strikes and strikebreakers, and people are hurt or killed. The book ends flatly and bleakly, with no fading action. It starts in the middle of the struggle; it ends in the middle of the struggle, with all the political theorizing embodied in the speeches and confrontations between the characters. The author never once intrudes into the book. Based on an actual event in the San Joaquin Valley in California, *In Dubious Battle* has the feel of a newspaper report.

As in *Tortilla Flat,* the characters are simple, even one dimensional, but this simplicity adds to the narrative force and is necessary to the theme. The basic needs of all men are the same. Only the economic system alienates one from the other.

Steinbeck's greatest literary triumphs were to come: the short novel *Of Mice and Men* (1937) and the much more sustained *Grapes of Wrath* (1939). The former is simpler. The men in *Of Mice and Men* are Lennie Small and George Milton. The latter is of normal intelligence, but the former, although physically strong, is mentally weak. He likes to touch small furry animals, such as rabbits and mice; George takes care that Lennie does not harm these animals. Together they dream of buying a small farm on cheap land.

These are primitive people reduced to the starkest of characterizations. Now stock figures, they were not so in 1937 when the book appeared. The Salinas Valley, which up until that time had not been explored in fiction, made the characters seem even fresher. If a crucial seduction scene in a barn was a cliché even in 1937, it is saved because it goes so horribly awry, as the best laid plans of mice and men often do, and as George and Lennie's plans do. That is the buried implication of the title, from Robert Burns's poem "To a Mouse."

Of Mice and Men is a novel with scenes blocked out as for a play, with each chapter taking place in one location. Plainly, Steinbeck had one eye on the theatrical possibilities when he composed it. Indeed, his almost immediate dramatization, staged on Broadway, with Broderick Crawford in the role of Lennie and Wallace Ford as George, was a great hit. It was played 207 times and won the New York Drama Critics' Circle Award.

In addition to of *Mice and Men* and *The Grapes of wrath*, Steinbeck wrote two more considerable novels. *Cannery Row* is a comic story in the manner of *Tortilla Flat* about the love of working-class people for the owner of a biological lab in Monterey. *East of Eden,* a historical novel set mostly in Salinas Valley, California, covers the period of 1890 to just after World War I and tells the story of one brother who is able to break away from a family life filled with recrimination and hurt to "rule over sin" as God promised Cain he could do in a land "east of Eden."

Both of these books furthered Steinbeck's reputation. He won the Nobel Prize for literature in 1962, the seventh American to do so. He took special pride in the award, writing to a friend that he had had "a long-time feud [with] the cutglass critics, that grey priesthood which defines literature and has little to do with reading."

The era of modernism had come to an end.

World War II

President Franklin D. Roosevelt (1882–1945), elected in 1932 when the Great Depression was ravaging the country, was a great innovator of social policy. Social security, many federal agencies still active today, and a more active social role for the government were his legacy. Roosevelt's most immediate motivation for starting these programs was the struggling economy, and in a small, somewhat patchwork way his efforts made a difference. Perhaps as important as his programs were Roosevelt's hopeful attitude and vital, engaging personality. However, more crucial than any of these factors was WORLD WAR II.

Nazism was only a movement, not a force, until 1933, when Hitler became chancellor of Germany. In a series of aggressive military and political moves, Adolf Hitler (1889–1945) started on his quest to rule Europe, even as Japan began its plans for increasing its territory in the East. Although theoretically neutral, the United States would find it even more difficult to stay out of this world war than it had World War I. The need to manufacture munitions, planes, tanks, guns, boats, and other items necessary to fight this war, one waged on both European and Asian fronts, brought an end to the Great Depression.

In 1918, the country was divided on the appropriateness of America taking part in a European conflict. Few such doubts existed by the time the Japanese bombed Pearl Harbor on December 7, 1941. That action made the mandate plain. In Europe, the actions of Adolf Hitler were so evidently the work of a cruel tyrant that no defense seemed possible.

Even today Hitler's atrocities seem unbelievable. Most notorious

> ### ▪ ▪ MOBILIZING FOR ▪ ▪ WORLD WAR II
>
> **Fighting a war on two fronts required a massive national effort. The entire country was put in the service of the U.S. military. It was during this time that such figures as Rosie the Riveter appeared. Rosie was a strong, capable-looking woman, showing her biceps, who adorned posters, encouraging women to take on jobs previously occupied by men who had gone to fight in Europe. "We can do it!" was her motto—and "we" meant the women and the United States.**
>
> **Wartime uses were found for peacetime machines. For example, a company that made machines to fill bottles with soda pop was converted to wartime use by adapting conveyor belts that held glass bottles to hold shell casings for artillery; the same machine that filled bottles with carbonated water and sugar now delivered a more explosive substance: gunpowder.**

was his wish to exterminate an entire race—the Jewish people. Economic conditions following World War I in Germany had been harsh. Inflation was so high that it took almost a wheelbarrow full of German banknotes to buy a loaf of bread. Based on misguided economic theorizing and personal beliefs stemming from a deep-seated psychosis, Hitler blamed the Jews for the economic troubles in Germany—and for many of its other social problems as well.

Hitler rounded up Jewish people in towns throughout Germany and the territories it conquered or annexed—Poland, Czechoslovakia, Austria—and simply shot them or shipped them to labor camps at Auschwitz, Bergen-Belsen, and other places, where the able-bodied were worked until they died, and women, children, and the sick were herded immediately into ovens and gassed. Six million Jews perished. The cruelties of the Nazis' treatment of the Jews is called the HOLOCAUST. European nations, aware of Hitler as an evil man, though possibly unaware of just how evil he was, mobilized in 1939. Soon America was engaged in the war against Hitler as well.

Embarking on such an ambitious project as fighting a war on two fronts required the mobilization of troops and the manufacturing of weapons, clothing, tanks, ships, airplanes, and machinery—a vast array of goods to support troops and provide them with what they needed in order to fight. It required massive infusions of capital, some of which came from the government. Although Roosevelt's federal works projects poured millions of dollars into the economy, World War II required billions more. It was this that lifted the nation out of the Great Depression.

Scott Fitzgerald characterized the 1920s as an "age of miracles, an age of art, an age of excess, an age of satire." The 1930s was the exact opposite: an age of ordinariness, social activism, restraint, and earnestness. The first half of the 1940s was another contrast: an age of war. In times such as those the country was united, notwithstanding its internal struggles, as it seldom has been in its history. The whole nation felt the necessity of defeating Hitler and the Japanese.

While stirring world events occupied the minds of most Americans, the same strains of thought and

▪ ▪ AFRICAN AMERICANS ▪ ▪
IN WORLD WAR II

Throughout the history of the United States, African Americans have served in the military but not always alongside whites. World War II was the last war, however, in which the races were segregated. The government held back from full integration, unwilling, for instance, to let African American nurses minister to white soldiers or vice versa.

In 1941, in response to a rising tide of protests, an all-black aviation school at Booker T. Washington's Tuskegee Institute was established. The school's squadron #99 was sent to North Africa where the 79th was engaged in fighting. Its distinguished performance and the cooperation between the two units was one of the first steps in integrating the armed forces. The leader of the 99th was Captain Benjamin O. Davis, who later became the first African American Air Force general.

In 1948, by which time Richard Wright had moved to Paris, President Truman signed an executive order officially integrating the military. Some soldiers returning from the war still faced the difficult life in the South described by Richard Wright in *Black Boy*, but for those who remained in the service, conditions were improving, if slowly.

culture as had characterized the Harlem Renaissance and the 1930s continued, albeit in somewhat less highlighted circumstances. The American writer whose career most exactly coincided with the period of World War II was Richard Wright.

Richard Wright (1908–1960)

A self-educated African American from Mississippi, Richard Wright in literary technique was a naturalist, who objectively recorded facts, with minimal authorial interference. Like many writers of the Harlem Renaissance, Wright was a communist, although he grew increasingly disenchanted with the Communist Party throughout the course of his life. After winning a prize from *Story* magazine for his first collection, *Uncle Tom's Children* (1938), Wright produced the two works for which he is best known, *Native Son* (1940) and *Black Boy* (1945).

Native Son is Bigger Thomas, a boy raised in the slums of Chicago. The novel is divided into three ominously named sections: "Fear," "Flight," and "Fate." "Fear" shows the slum life of Bigger Thomas, including an incident in which a vicious rat with yellow teeth bites Bigger before he kills it violently.

This violence is a prelude to more. Employed by a rich white family, Bigger finds himself carrying a drunken daughter upstairs to put her to bed. The woman moans—the scene is filled with sexual innuendo—and Bigger tries to stifle her moans by covering her face with a pillow, accidentally suffocating her. He ineptly tries to cover up what he has done. Then he rapes and kills his girlfriend. The police track Bigger to a rooftop, beat him savagely, and throw him in jail. A trial seals his fate.

Native Son exposes the psychological tragedy of African Americans as Wright understands it. One death was an accident, but the second was motivated by Bigger's being forced into a position where his only choice was to rebel and to become that which people did not want him to be. He wants what he is not supposed to have because he has been denied it so long there is no other way to define himself. "What I killed for, I am."

An intensely exciting novel, *Native Son* is pessimistic about the possibilities for an African American to live in the country of his birth. After writing a popular account of his nomadic youth, *Black Boy,* Wright moved to Paris. A decade of novel writing from abroad followed, but the 1950s were a time of the Cold War, when communists were seen as America's major enemy. His later books never

■ ■ ■ ■ ■ HIDDEN ANGER IN ■ ■ ■ ■ ■
RICHARD WRIGHT

In "Alas, Poor Richard," from *Nobody Knows My Name* (1961), James Baldwin (1924–1987) discusses the violence in Richard Wright's work. He says that Wright's violence

> is gratuitous and compulsive . . . because the root of the violence is never examined. The root is rage. It is the rage, almost literally the howl, of a man who is being castrated . . . . When in Wright's pages a Negro male is found hacking a white woman to death, the very gusto with which this is done, and the great attention paid to the details of physical destruction reveal a terrible attempt to break out of the cage in which the American imagination has placed him for so long.

Baldwin's understanding owes something to the psychoanalytical theories of Freud. He sees beyond the immediate motivation ascribed to Bigger Thomas in Wright's novel to a psychological pattern in the author, Richard Wright, and he ascribes to it a primal, sexual cause. Moreover, Baldwin generalizes further by implying that white America has imprisoned black men and is at the root of the violence visited on it. This kind of analysis is symptomatic of an increasing radicalization of African American thought. Wright's imagination spoke powerfully to the generation that followed him, especially to social critics such as Baldwin.

had the impact of *Native Son* and *Black Boy,* but Wright was, until his death, one of the major African American voices.

Hiroshima

Richard Wright's two major books appeared in the first and last years of America's involvement in World War II. Although memorable novels emerged from that war—Norman Mailer's (1923–2007) *The Naked and the Dead* (1948) and *From Here to Eternity* (1951) by James Jones (1921–1977)—it was John Hersey's (1914–1993) *Hiroshima* (1946) at the very end of the war that signaled the start of the new era and of the Cold War itself. The event with which Hersey was concerned was the dropping of the first atomic bomb on the city of Hiroshima in Japan "at exactly fifteen minutes past eight in the morning, on August 6, 1945, Japanese time," as the account notes with dry precision.

The original publication of *Hiroshima* was remarkable for breaking tradition. *The New Yorker,* a magazine based in New York City and whose primary readers were sophisticates, devoted a whole issue to John Hersey's report. *The New Yorker* had, in the 1940s, and still has today, a reputation for irony and detachment, for being able to take any event in stride. Centering the entire magazine on *Hiroshima* indicated that this was an event that was outside the normal bounds of experience.

Through four chapters, "A Noiseless Flash," "The Fire," "Details Are Being Investigated," and "Panic Grass and Feverview," the book follows the lives of six ordinary citizens: Toshiko Saski, a clerk in a tin factory; Masakazu Fujii, a doctor; Hatsuyo Nakamura, the widow of a tailor; Father Wilhelm Kleinsorge, a German Jesuit priest living in Japan; Dr. Terufumi Sasaki, a surgeon in a Red Cross Hospital; and Kiyoshi Tanimoto, a Methodist pastor. Hersey is not interested in their background, only in what they were doing at the moment the bomb dropped.

Their lives had been affected by the war, but what occurred that August day was so different that they were left in utter confusion. Hatsuyo Nakamura, for example, had become used to air raid sirens, and, not hearing anything, she decided to let her children sleep a little longer rather than taking them to a shelter. The bomb, however, is a "noiseless flash," so that she is unprepared. Father Kleinsorge sensibly tried to relate what was happening to his own knowledge and consequently concluded a bomb had fallen on him and that bombs were like meteor collisions on the earth. Toshiko

Native son, 1943
Richard Wright, photographed by Gordon Parks. Wright's books deal with race, sex, and politics.

▪ ▪ ▪ ▪ ▪ How $E = mc^2$ Shook ▪ ▪ ▪ ▪ ▪
the World

The dropping of the atomic bomb and the new era it began had their origins in the ideas of Albert Einstein (1879–1955), whose understanding of physics changed the way scientists understood reality.

Before Einstein, most scientists accepted the universe of Sir Isaac Newton (1642–1727), in which space and time existed independently of the world. They were absolutes. In a series of radical papers, as upsetting to science as modernism was to literature, Einstein showed this idea to be false. Space and time are relative to each other. If you and your friend are wearing identical watches and your friend remains on the ground while you fly in a very fast airplane around the world, when you land, your watch will be a tiny fraction of a second slower. Time is not constant, and another absolute had been removed from the universe.

A further implication of Einstein's thought was that mass and energy depend on each other: $E = mc^2$. This equation, although not in itself a moral challenge, led to the creation of the atomic bomb, a weapon so horrific that it appalled even the man whose thinking enabled it. It permitted "manunkind," in Cummings's memorable coinage, to take control of enormous forces by applying the idea that a decrease in mass means a concomitant release of energy, as when a uranium atom is split and loses its mass. Einstein, a pacifist, was as stunned as John Hersey by the devastation that proceeded from $E = mc^2$.

Saski was thrown to the ground, her leg twisted under her and crushed, ironically, by a bookcase. The peaceful things of human knowledge have turned into weapons.

Hersey's detached style contrasts to the anguish and horrors he reports. Father Kleinsorge wants to take water in a teapot he borrows. He gets lost in the underbrush and finds twenty men who want something to drink. "Their faces were wholly burned, their eye-sockets were hollow, the fluid from their melted eyes had run down their cheeks. . . . Their mouths were mere swollen, pus-covered wounds, which they could not bear to stretch enough to admit the spout of the teapot." After some friends tell Toshiko Saski that her family is all dead, they leave her to die. Later, men find her and re-move the bookcase under which she has lain for two days and two nights. She "had become convinced that she was dulled to pain" but found that she was not. When one of the men touches her legs, she faints.

The last chapter of *Hiroshima* (as originally published; in 1985 Hersey added a fifth) is grimly ironic. The radiation from the bomb has caused the plants to flower, and the city is awash in a "vivid, lush, optimistic green." Those who survived the bomb get radia-tion sickness. Father Kleinsorge is weak; his white blood cell count fluctuates wildly. Dr. Sasaki has hemorrhaging spots on his skin. Hatsuyo Nakamura's hair falls out. Although these victims eventu-ally do recover, others do not.

Japanese scientists examine the area close to where the bomb hit. They find that the light was so intense it burned shad-ows into those buildings that survived. Although the scientists are awed, "a surprising number of people of Hiroshima remained more or less indifferent about the ethics of using the bomb." This point Hersey does not directly address either. He closes with the account of a schoolboy who lived through the blast. The day be-fore he had gone swimming. Then the bomb hit and people were walking around bleeding. He knew two girls who looked for their mothers, but their mothers were dead. It is as though all these events, some ordinary and some so horrific as to be beyond imagination, were equivalent.

With *Hiroshima* a new era began, an era of warfare even more terrifying than World War I, with which the modernist period opened. In Hersey's account it is an event so horrific it defies comment.

7. The Great Depression (1929–1939)—The Years that Defined an Era

The effects of the years of the GREAT DEPRESSION were evident in all walks of American life—in literature, music, art. Whatever the causes of the Great Depression—the severe economic crisis of the 1930s, which supposedly began with the stock market crash on Wall Street in 1929—the years from 1929 to 1939 were ones of unprecedented hardship and fear, not only for more than 25% of the U.S. population who were unemployed but also for family members or those who knew neighbors facing these hardships.

The loss of jobs affected both urban and rural America. The domino effect—one failure affecting another, then another, and so on—from unemployment caused layers of jobs to disappear because in a community without jobs, no matter its size, the ability to buy from and sell to neighbors eroded. In the cities, long lines formed whenever "Now Hiring" signs appeared, and even longer lines were seen in front of charitable soup kitchens. Families who could afford to do so moved in together; however, by the early 1930s, "HOOVERVILLES," temporary camps of tents and cardboard shacks, sprang up around many cities. Many of the inhabitants were men looking for work, but families who had nowhere to go were also part of the population.

In the country, a farmer who could not pay the mortgage faced eviction and homelessness. In addition, SHARECROPPERS, who may have worked for a landowner who was planning to take the rented land out of production, lost their homes and their livelihoods. Although some managed barely to get by, many joined a growing exodus of migrants. Whereas the South was hit hard, parts of the Midwest, particularly the plains of Oklahoma, were devastated by yet another disaster—drought and the resulting DUST BOWL. The area known as the Dust Bowl was marked by thousands of ruined acres of farmland, a situation that forced entire townships of farm families to migrate elsewhere. Fear of the future pervaded the country, and the writers, artists, musicians, journalists, and photographers of the era reflect this turmoil in their work.

In 1935, President Franklin Delano Roosevelt established the WORKS PROGRESS ADMINISTRATION (WPA) to help generate jobs. The U.S. government also funded a FEDERAL WRITERS' PROJECT, which

■ ■ ■ ■ BUYING ON MARGIN ■ ■ ■ ■

In the 1920s (as today, with some differences), many investors bought stocks on MARGIN. They put up only a fraction of the price in anticipation of a rising market. If I buy x for $10 and it rises to $20, I have doubled my money. If I buy x for $2, "borrowing" $8, and it rises to $20 I have increased my money tenfold, less interest charges. That is buying "on margin."

Generally speaking, for the most part, prices in the 1920s did rise. People with very small incomes had margin portfolios worth millions. F. Scott Fitzgerald wrote a story about one, a barber richer than his customers.

However, if the price of the stock falls far and fast, those who bought on margin will be asked to come up with funds to cover the loss because their "loans" will be in jeopardy. They may be forced to sell to cover the loss and lose all their investments.

Sometimes prices fall so fast that purchasers cannot cover their losses even by selling. Then the market has to absorb bankruptcies. If enough people go bankrupt, the market itself collapses. That is what happened in October 1929. It happened not only in the United States but also globally. Resulting devaluations of currency in Europe caused wide-ranging social unrest.

was formed to find work for unemployed white-collar workers, including editors, writers, researchers, and art critics. The program employed more than six thousand men and women from its beginning in 1935 until World War II ended the need for such jobs. Saul Bellow, Ralph Ellison, Zora Neale Hurston, Arthur Miller, John Steinbeck, Orson Welles, and Richard Wright were among some of the most famous writers who gained assistance from this project. Many who were perhaps less talented worked instead as field workers for about $80 a month and produced valuable oral histories from these experiences. The best known is *Born in Slavery: Slave Narratives from the Federal Writers' Program 1936–1938,* which records more than two thousand firsthand accounts of slavery. Most of the writing is simple description, for example state guides explaining local history and significant locations, but the best remembered writers vividly depict the despair and anger in Depression-era REALISM.

The Grapes of Wrath

John Steinbeck's *Grapes of Wrath* (1939) is the iconic novel of those years portraying characters and situations derived from rural poverty.

It is an epic that recapitulates the American movement west under harsh circumstances. The Joads—Grampa and Granma, Uncle John, Pa and Ma, Tom, Noah, Connie and his wife Rose-of-Sharon, and their children—live in the Dust Bowl of Oklahoma, which is described from a general overview. The novel is at pains to keep its focus on community rather than on one central figure, as community is Steinbeck's key value.

Conditions are harsh in the Dust Bowl for people and animals. In a famous chapter, Steinbeck describes a turtle crossing a highway. A truck hits the turtle, almost killing it, but the turtle spins to the side of the road and lands on its back, eventually making its way to its destination. The impersonality of mechanical contrivances, such as the truck, and their indifference to life resemble the tractors that pull the machines that drive the Joads away from their work on the land. Like the automobiles sold by dealers to poor people desperate for any means of transportation, they are dilapidated and mechanically defective: cars that are prone to break down like the national economy itself. They are extensions of the banking interests that finance them and that control the economic life that is so harsh to poor families like the Joads.

Ma Joad, the strongest member of the family, holds the group together through her strength of will and common sense, but the Joads are worse off at the end of the story, after arriving in California, than they were at the beginning: Their son Tom has gone, their number is diminished, and their plight is more desperate. This mood corresponds to the deepest feelings of the nation during Great Depression. The publication of *The Grapes of Wrath* in 1939 summed up the decade.

The book also signified for a time the end of a belief in the American dream of hard work and rewards. Believers in that dream, such as Fitzgeraid, did not like Steinbeck's work, and Hemingway, with his focus on aesthetics, also did not find it to his taste. Steinbeck, of course, did not write for them and independently pursued his own ideas.

Lyrics of Woody Guthrie (1912–1967)

Not only was the plight of the Okies, farm families from the Oklahoma dust bowl, revealed in literature, but also by Woody Guthrie, a popular folksinger who performed on network radio and

Migrant worker stalled in the desert, 1937
Although this car is in better condition than the one the Joads used to travel
westward in *The Grapes of Wrath*, the photo captures the hardness of the life
of the period, the discriminating appraisal needed to succeed on such journeys,
and the long distances involved.

at political rallies. He wrote his song "Tom Joad" to honor both Steinbeck's character from his novel *The Grapes of Wrath* and the hundreds of thousands of migrant Okies whose story he understood. Guthrie sympathized with the underdog, and no group was more maligned than the Okies who migrated to California. Although Steinbeck visited and interviewed those in the farm camps before writing his novel, Guthrie lived and traveled with them. By traveling and sleeping with migrant families and hobos, he learned their stories firsthand and absorbed the mood of the impoverished workers. The lyrics for "Tom Joad"(1940), written shortly after the publication of Steinbeck's novel, reflect the bitterness, despair, and pride of those migrants:

> Us workin' folkses, all get together
> 'Cause we ain't got a chance anymore.

Guthrie identifies with their belief in themselves and with the bitterness they feel for having been abandoned by other Americans and the system.

The titles of some of Guthrie's other songs written in the 1930s also mirror his experiences with the Dust Bowl refugees. "Dust Storm Disaster" and "Talkin' Dust Bowl Blues" brought vivid images of the disaster to those in the city, people who had only heard of the farm evictions as part of the general economic failures. Guthrie shared his songs in taverns, camps along his route, and eventually over the air on KFVD radio in Los Angeles. He sang about the reality of 50-mile-per-hour winds blowing away the topsoil—the land no longer held down by grass or wheat. The driving winds choked livestock and those unfortunate enough to be without shelter. Guthrie's lyrics described days as dark as nights, with a blood red sun; he sang of the hopelessness of those who had to leave their ruined homesteads. After these experiences in California, Guthrie moved to New York and eventually joined the Almanac Singers, a group that popularized his songs and ideas. He maintained his belief in helping the downtrodden until his death from a genetic nerve disease in 1967, never giving up the hope that, "This land was made for you and me."

A City and the Great Depression

Hunger did not exist only on the Dust Bowl farms and in the migrant camps. Richard Wright's autobiography, initially titled *American Hunger* but published instead as *Black Boy* (1945), takes him from the rural South to Chicago just as the Depression begins. He had battled hunger most of his life, even as a child.

▪ ▪ ▪ ▪ DUST BOWL HARDSHIPS FOR THE OKIES ▪ ▪ ▪ ▪

The term *Dust Bowl* refers to the Great Plains in the center of the United States, from the Dakotas down through Texas. This area was extensively farmed, and for years farmers planted wheat and other crops, which grew bountifully. This was also the era of the big farm, with thousands of acres.

In the 1930s, however, weather patterns changed, and agribusiness planting practices led to disaster. There was an extensive drought, and no crops would grow. Without the roots of vegatation to hold down the soil, the winds that blew across the plains lifted acres of valuable topsoil and scattered it as dust. It drifted like snow because there was nothing to anchor it. No conservation measures had been taken.

The dust storms continued to rage throughout the 1930s. In response, thousands of American farmers from the states of Oklahoma, Texas, Arkansas, Kansas, Nebraska, and Iowa moved westward to California in search of a better life. Farmers left not only because they could not cultivate their barren land, but also because their homes were seized by the banks in foreclosures. This exodus of farmers during the Dust Bowl was one of the largest migrations in American history, with at least 2.5 million people leaving the Great Plains region. Although the migrants came from many states of the Great Plains, they were collectively known as "Okies."

Smaller farmers could not survive. They had no resources, so many, like the Joads in *The Grapes of Wrath*, packed up what they could salvage and left. These impoverished farmers were scorned. (The folksinger Woody Guthrie wrote songs about their plight.) Staying at a migrant labor camp, the Joads and their friends get their first taste of discrimination when they are called "Okies." "Okie use' ta mean you was from Oklahoma," they are told. "Now it means you're a dirty son-of-a-bitch. Okie means you're scum."

Hunger had always been more or less at my elbow when I played, but now I began to wake up at night to find hunger standing at my bedside, staring at me gauntly. The hunger I had known before this had been no grim, hostile stranger; it had been a normal hunger that when I ate a crust or two I was satisfied. But this new hunger baffled me, scared me, made me angry and insistent.

Arriving in Chicago in December 1927, Wright found he was too underweight to work in the post office, despite having passed the written examination. A crash diet to gain weight proved successful, and he was hired in 1929 only to be let go within the year, when the volume of mail diminished as a result of the Depression. He moved his mother and brother, for whom he was the sole provider, from one small apartment to another, unable to get steady work except for the occasional odd job cleaning the gutters of Chicago. Finally, when his mother told him there was no food, he applied for public welfare:

> I sat waiting for hours, resentful of the mass of hungry people about me . . . As I waited I became aware of something happening in the room. The black men and women were mumbling quietly among themselves; they had not known one another before they had come here, but now their timidity and shame were wearing off and they were exchanging experiences.

Despite the hunger and humiliation, the shared experience in that situation brought Wright some sense of community, a reaction seen in many works from that era.

Among other groups, however, Wright found hostility. Still in Chicago, Wright attended his first unit meeting of the Communists, a group he admired because, "Negro equality was one of the main tenets of Communism." There he found that members of his own race distrusted him because of his writing and had classified him as an intellectual, meaning he might be disloyal or untrustworthy to the ideals of the Party:

> I discovered that it was not wise to be seen reading books that had not been endorsed by the Communist party. On one occasion I was asked to show a book that I carried under my arm. The comrade looked at it and shook his head. . . . "You know," he said, his voice dropping to a low, confidential tone, "many comrades go wrong by reading books of the bourgeoisie. The party in the Soviet Union had trouble with people like you." . . . An invisible wall was building slowly between me and the people with whom I had cast my lot . . . I had to win the confidence of people who had been misled so often that they were afraid of anybody who differed from themselves. Yet deep down I feared their militant ignorance.

At first championed by the Communist party, Wright eventually was expelled from it, in part, because of the way he portrayed its machinations in his most significant work of fiction, *Native Son*

Dust Storm

Writers such as John Steinbeck, Josephine W. Johnson, and Karen Hesse wrote about the stark challenges presented to hard-working people by external forces such as nature, society, and fate. In response to the devasting poverty and homelessness created by the powerful Dust Bowl storms similar to the one seen approaching Stratford, Texas, in this 1935 photograph, desperate farmers and other workers were forced to leave their homes in search of jobs, dignity, and deliverance.

• • • • THE "ABRAHAM LINCOLN BRIGADE": • • • •
AMERICANS IN SPAIN

From 1936 to 1939, a small interesting group of U.S. citizens took part in the Spanish Civil War, most of them fighting with Republican forces against the Fascist militias of Francisco Franco. Although often remembered as the "Abraham Lincoln Brigade," the Americans fighting in Spain actually formed two different battalions, one named for Lincoln, and the other for George Washington. These Americans joined with others from Europe and Latin America as part of the International Brigade, fighting for what they originally believed to be the rights of the people.

The political and philosophic divisions among the Spanish, as well as among those who went to help one side or the other, ran a wide range of beliefs. Spain had been a Republic, but a significant number of landowners, businessmen, military, and, especially, Roman Catholic clerics did not approve of the government's lenient policies toward labor groups, small farmers, and intellectuals who wanted the general population to have more influence. This division set the stage for extremes on both sides: monarchists who wanted the stability and tradition of a strong, single leader, and anarchists who wanted no restrictions, believing that any government would eventually fall to the power of the people. Between these two extremes lay multiple splinter groups, but internationally, three sovereign nations took sides, despite a general declaration of non-interference on the part of most nations. Nazi Germany, under Hitler and Mussolini's Fascist Italy, supported the Nationalists, while the Union of Soviet Socialist Republics, under Stalin, supported the Republicans. As the Spanish Civil War progressed, the Abraham Lincoln Brigade was often caught up in the plans and goals of the communists, both those of the Russians and those with international hopes. To make matters even more complicated, the Russian communists themselves were split between those who followed Stalin and those who followed Trotsky, Stalin's rival.

With these starkly conflicting ideas, it is not surprising that the Republic's side in the fighting suffered many defeats. Historians now realize that Hitler was using these battles as a trial run for his plans to wage war throughout Europe. He supplied aircraft, tanks, and artillery that massively outgunned what the Republicans had. The first real violence had broken out in 1936 when General Franco led a well-planned uprising centered in military camps, and the regular military kept the upper hand throughout the fighting, especially with the armaments supplied by Germany. Even though the Abraham Lincoln Brigade took part in several battles, they did not accomplish much in the way of military success. Eventually, France denied Americans permission to enter Spain through its border, and in the spring of 1938, most of the Americans were told to leave with the international arm of the Communist Party in Russia taking charge of the International Brigade.

To some Americans, joining the Brigade was considered an act of bravery for a good cause; but to the U.S. government, Soviet involvement and the fear of communism of any kind made those who went to Spain or who supported them suspect. President Franklin Roosevelt's attorney general indicted several individuals who had recruited young men to go to Spain as disloyal to the United States. Those recruited had included college students who believed in the cause, as well as the unemployed who sought food and clothing.

However, grave questions remained as to what political group was really in charge of the military and political operation. Even in the field, the question as to the final goals of those in charge of the fight became less clear. John Dos Passos' *Adventures of a Young Man* (1939) and Ernest Hemingway's *For Whom the Bell Tolls* (1940) made the complex, grim reality seem adventuresome and romantic. The singer Paul Robeson supported the American members of the Brigade by visiting and speaking about the young men's fight against fascism. One prominent medical group funded and staffed a field hospital. However, with the increasing influence of the Soviets and the military success of the Nationalist rebel army, American idealism faced the reality of defeat along with the disturbing questions as to the ultimate goals of those fighting on the Republican side. Those goals became irrelevant, however, when the Nationalists seized power, and General Franco held that power as dictator until his death in 1975. At that time, a descendent of the Bourbon monarchy was named king. However, the current government, based on a constitution established in 1978, has an elected Congress and President. A few of those still living, individuals who had left America in the Depression years to fight for a democratic cause, have seen the intervening years accomplish what they failed to do.

(1940). As he would later say in his autobiography, "If this country can't find its way to a human path, if it can't inform conduct with a deep sense of life, then all of us, black as well as white, are going down the same drain. . . ." To Wright, the Depression years deepened the realities of racism and poverty.

Studs Terkel (1912–2008)

As Wright survived the Great Depression in Chicago as part of the Federal Writers' Project, Studs Terkel also joined the radio division of the same Chicago project and, almost by accident, ended up reading a part from one of the scripts he had written. From there, he performed in radio soap operas and on WAIT radio news. By the end of World War II, Terkel was a regular on Chicago radio, and by 1955, he became known for his interviews in which an amazing variety of Americans answered questions about their lives. His easygoing style and genuine interest in their ideas produced interviews that have opened the window into the amazing range of experiences that came from the Depression years. He published these interviews in his book *Hard Times* (1970), a title that deliberately echoes that of Charles Dickens' grim 1854 novel about the industrialization of England.

Hard Times

The memories and reactions of these men and women clarify the extraordinary influence those years had on those who lived through them. The interviews in *Hard Times* range from stories of those who had been successes to those who found themselves destitute. For example, financier Arthur A. Robertson said he made a fortune buying businesses from banks when their owners could not pay what they owed. He called himself a "scavenger" because, he explained, "I used to buy broken-down businesses that banks took over. That was one of my best eras of prosperity." He further described Wall Street quite casually:

> In 1929, it was strictly a gambling casino with loaded dice. The few sharks taking advantage of the multitude of suckers . . . I saw shoeshine boys buying $50,000 worth of stock with $500 down. Everything was bought on hope. . . . That was really responsible for the collapse.

Terkel also interviewed a Chicago policeman with a very different perspective, a man who remembered having worked for American Express before he was laid off in 1933. He explained that

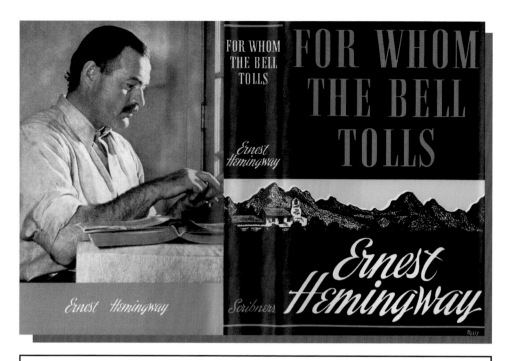

For Whom the Bell Tolls by Ernest Hemingway
Set in the second year of the Spanish Civil War, Hemingway's novel centers
on American Robert Jordan's assignment to help blow up a bridge to harass
Franco's Fascist armies. Jordan fights alongside Spanish resistance fighters
who back a democratic solution for Spain. In the next decades, Americans who
fought for the Spanish Republic ironically came under suspicion as being partial
to communism.

he was unable to get work for more than a year; when he did get the job on the Chicago police force, he had to buy his own uniform, guns, and shirts on a salary of $2,300 a year. He also remembered going to work on the streetcar, as did 95% of the other officers. He explained to Terkel the difference between life in the 1930s and what it was like after World War II when he stated that "most everyone now is living beyond their means."

In another section titled "Sixteen Ton," Terkel interviewed coal miners, hearing about the lack of safety in the mines, the long hours they worked under ground, and how, during the Depression, the company store kept families in debt by increasing the prices they charged. The conflict described in the coal mines between labor and management during the Depression is similar to the interviews in the "Three Strikes" section of *Hard Times*. Mike Widman, in describing Ford Motors' work rules, said that bathroom breaks were allowed only with permission of the foreman and often were denied. If someone was two minutes late, he was docked a full hour's pay, and if it happened three times, he was fired. He goes on to that say men in plain clothes, called the service department, were part of a surveillance team who looked for what were called "trouble makers," those who were trying to organize for a union. "Many of them were ex-cons," he told Terkel.

In the same section, Dr. Lewis Andreas, who founded Chicago's first medical center with group practice and low fees, saw police firing on unarmed strikers during a strike at Republic Steel in 1937:

> The Wagner Act had become the law—the right of labor to picket, to organize . . . Nobody was armed. But the police got the idea these people were armed . . . All of a sudden I heard some popping . . . About three minutes later, they started bringing in the wounded, shot. There were about fifty shot. Ten of them died. One little boy was shot in the heel. I took care of him. One woman was shot in the arm.

Terkel, like Wright, had trouble with the local Communists because, he believed, they wanted all the credit for helping the strikers. Dr. Andreas described most of the Party members as having no tolerance for others' ideas and also being without humor.

Labor unrest was not limited to the industrial sector but broke out in the rural areas, too. Terkel's interview with César Chávez, the president of the United Farm Workers of America, reveals problems of greed, racism, and the resulting need to organize. Chávez recounts

how the Chávez family, father and uncles, had owned their farms
north of Yuma, Arizona, for two generations when, in 1936, the bank
refused the federal government's guarantee of their loans. The bank
president owned the land around the farms and did not allow any
guarantees on loans for the farms he personally had bought up. The
Chávez family climbed into their Chevy and drove to California:

> We were pretty new. We had never been migratory workers. We
> were taken advantage of quite a bit by the labor contractor and
> the crew pusher [specialist in finding cheap farm labor] . . . labor
> strikes were everywhere. We were one of the strikingest families,
> I guess. My father didn't like the conditions and he would begin
> to agitate . . . If we were picking on a piece rate and we knew
> they were cheating on the weight, we wouldn't stand for it. So
> we'd lose the job, and we'd go elsewhere . . . We were trapped.

Chávez also remembered how many times he saw signs in little
diners that said, "White Trade Only," and how many waitresses refused even to sell his family coffee for their own pot because they
were "Mexican."

Terkel also interviewed those who had been the most destitute.
Louis Banks spent years wandering and looking for work, explaining
from his bed in a veterans' hospital, "A man had to be on the road.
Had to leave his wife, . . . tryin' to send her money, worryin' how
she's starving." He said that he felt shame and was so glad when
he could put on a uniform and join the army when the war came.
He added in the interview that he would rather be in the army than
in another Depression. Terkel's interview with Frank Czerwonka
shows another, more violent side of being on the road. No longer a
hobo but a salaried garbage collector after World War II, Czerwonka
and his family had run illegal speakeasies during Prohibition. By the
time he was in his twenties, he wanted out of that life; therefore, in
1931, he jumped on the back of a train with 7 cents and his lunch
as his only possessions:

> Freight trains were amazing in them days. When a train would
> stop in a small town and the bums got off, the population
> tripled . . . Women even, and quite a few were tryin' to dis-
> guise themselves. Oh, there were some mean people travelin'
> around . . . this bit about the code that the old bums had broke
> down. If it was still being used, they weren't letting the
> newcomers know—the nouveau paupers.

▪ ▪ ▪ ▪ THE FARM STRIKES IN THE MIDWEST ▪ ▪ ▪ ▪

At the beginning of the Depression, job losses were greater in the cities than in rural areas. With the collapse of the stock market and subsequent bank failures, factories and businesses in the cities, which depended on bank loans to meet their payroll, closed their doors when loans were no longer available. As customers lost their jobs, the retail stores that sold them goods also lost income, and the downward spiral continued.

In contrast to this urban scenario, most farmers were, at first, in better shape than their city counterparts because they at least had food and shelter. Then, the terrible drought hit most of the Midwest and farmers' problems increased. The story of the Okies and the devastating dust storms have overshadowed other compelling dramas that occurred in those years in other states, where farmers were sometimes in opposition to each other as well as to those who marketed their product.

During the administration of President Herbert Hoover, when the federal government did not believe that its policies should impact the economic situation, some of the states and cities attempted to help those most affected by the downturn. A national conference of mayors tried to pressure the federal government for help, and some states did revert to state bank moratoriums to stop disastrous runs on the banks—when depositors withdrew their funds because there was no deposit insurance in those years. In Roosevelt's first one hundred days as president, he closed the banks in all states, had Congress pass a bill to help banks prevent such panics, and ended the banking crisis. A multitude of problems, however, still persisted, including a free fall in prices for farm goods.

In Wisconsin, the legislature enacted its own system of unemployment compensation, a model for later federal legislation, but that did not help the farmers who were self-employed. Because Wisconsin was the largest producer of milk and milk products in the country, with 63% of the land used for farming, the impact of the drop in prices was especially ruinous to dairy farmers who had seen milk prices fall by a third from 1929 to 1933. Whereas wholesalers could keep a large share of the profits, the actual producers got less and less. In addition, the dairies that produced milk for the major bottling companies were, for the most part, able to stay in business, but the farms that produced milk for the cheese and butter industry were paid at a lower rate. The inequity of this situation led to bitterness and even violence in the ensuing years.

The resulting conflict has been called a kind of civil war between the two kinds of dairy farmers; those selling milk for bottling refused to join the strikes called for by the farmers who produced milk for cheese and butter. At first, farm groups and cooperatives tried to coordinate their plans, but by 1933, those for the strike refused to sell their milk and set up roadblocks to stop those not striking from selling theirs. If a milk trucker refused to turn back, the strikers forcibly dumped the milk. Finding a way around the roadblocks became a strategy for those still selling milk until the striking farmers began tainting the delivered milk with kerosene. Finally, the state called in the National Guard, who used tear gas and even fixed bayonets to allow the trucks to get through. In May of that year, two teenagers were killed by a guardsman who shot them when they refused to stop their car. What may have seemed like a glorious adventure to help became a tragedy. A second fatal incident occurred when an elderly farmer fell, or was pushed, from a milk delivery truck when it left a roadblock. In October, in Wisconsin, the violence escalated as the two sets of farmers tried to force their own agendas. Seven creameries were bombed, thousands of pounds of milk were destroyed, and a 60-year-old farmer was shot by a passenger in a car as the farmer brought food to those on the roadblock. With no real success and millions of dollars lost in destroyed dairy products, the violence finally came to an end. One of the cooperatives bought up creameries to try and maintain prices, but the slowly improving economy was ultimately the most effective answer to the dairy farmers.

The federal government tried to help with a tactic that is considered wise economically but that caused a public outcry. To stop farmers from striking and to help them improve the prices they received, the Agricultural Adjustment Act of President Roosevelt's "New Deal" tried to raise prices by asking farmers to destroy their crops and livestock, as well as limit milk production. The theory was to reduce supply and therefore raise prices as the demand for those products remained the same. Nine basic crops were identified, and farmers were paid small amounts to maintain the limits. Limitations of milk production made only a small improvement in the incomes of dairy farmers in Wisconsin. However, pictures of pigs being killed and buried, along with crops being plowed under, infuriated those in the cities, where there were still long breadlines of the hungry.

Terkel's "Note," as part of his preface, says, "This being a book about Time as well as *a* time; for some the bell has tolled." *Hard Times* is a history of a multitude of memories from violence and despair to hope and longing; it is a personal perspective on the years that defined an era.

Contemporary Authors Use the Great Depression

Although the Great Depression historically ended with the beginning of World War II, modern authors have often used the period as a vehicle with which to tell a story, because compelling literature generally requires characters to face conflict in a compelling setting. Two Newberry Medalists award winners of young adult fiction selected the Depression era as the setting to challenge their characters. For example, Christopher Paul Curtis' *Bud, Not Buddy* (1999) and Karen Hesse's *Out of the Dust* (1997) take place in the 1930s. The first novel begins in Flint, Michigan, and the second is set in the panhandle of Oklahoma, part of the Dust Bowl during the Depression.

Bud, Not Buddy

In *Bud, Not Buddy*, set in the early 1930s, before Franklin Roosevelt's election, young Bud Caldwell's mother dies, and he is sent to an abusive foster home from which he escapes. He uses the local library as a temporary home for a while and takes advantage of the free meals given out at the bread lines, even though the lines go around the corner. Finally, he decides "to ride the rails" to get to the city, where he thinks the father he has never met lives. He and another runaway boy are advised to find Flint's Hooverville as a place from which to hitch a ride on a train. This cardboard shanty town has hundreds of people already assembled, waiting for the next train west, so Bud decides he is in the right place. Although he misses the train, he eventually hitchhikes to his destination. Curtis then uses an explanation from a helpful Hooverville resident as a history lesson to clarify why such shanty towns exist.

Out of the Dust

In Karen Hesse's *Out of the Dust,* set in the Oklahoma panhandle, Billie Jo faces her high school years through the tragedies of her mother's death and the devastation from the dust storms that literally wipe out all that is familiar to her. Written in free verse and taking place from January 1934 to December 1935, Hesse uses

■ ■ ■ ■ HOOVERVILLE FROM *BUD, NOT BUDDY* ■ ■ ■ ■

After the stock market crash in October 1929 and the devastating economic depression that followed, hundreds of thousands of workers across the country lost their jobs. People used whatever means they had to survive. In the 1930s, "Hoovervilles" sprang up in American cities, as homeless men, women, and children were forced to leave their homes and apartments. Destitute Americans, who had no other place to go, dubbed these groups of shacks "Hoovervilles" in "honor" of President Herbert Hoover. Ironically, when Hoover was elected president in 1928, the nation's economy appeared to be soaring. Sadly, Hoovervilles, each one no different from the rest, became a common sight from coast to coast

Explaining to Bud and his friend that they are in the right place, the man from Hooverville says:

> "Naw, son, what you're looking for is Hooverville, with a v, like in President Herbert Hoover . . . They're all over the country, this here is the Flint version." [Bud remembers] . . . the city was bigger than I thought it was. The raggedy little huts were in every direction you looked. And there were more people sitting around than I had first thought too, mostly it was men and big boys, but there were a couple of women now and then and kid or two. He went on, "All these people are just like you, they're tired, hungry and a little bit nervous about tomorrow. . . . It don't matter if you're looking for Chicago or Detroit or Orlando or Oklahoma City. I rode the rails to all of them. You might think or hear that things are better just down the line, but they're singing the sad song all over this country."

While those in the Flint Hooverville befriend the boys and share their food, the arrival of the Pinkerton railroad police to stop anyone from getting on the train is a frightening development for Bud and his friend. The conflict in this story has those trying to ride the rails outmaneuvering the police, even if Bud himself does not make the train. In reality, when those who had lost everything clashed with those who were trying to maintain what they still had, such confrontations often erupted into violence and sometimes ended in death.

powerful poetic images to let the reader experience the horror of the dust storms when families are forced to take shelter in school rooms, and drifts of dust even sift into cars and under the doors of houses:

> Six miles out of town the air turned cold,
> birds beat their wings
> everywhere you looked
> whole flocks
> dropping out of the sky
> crowding on fence posts.
> I was sulking in the truck beside my father
> when
> heaven's shadow crept across the plains,
> a black cloud
> big and silent as Montana
> boiling on the horizon and
> barreling toward us.
> More tumbled from the sky
> frantically keeping ahead of the dust.
> We watched as the storm swallowed the light
> . . . and the dust was on us.

The story includes Billie Jo's emotional and physical battle with the terrible accident that kills her mother and burns her own hands so severely that she can barely wash the dishes, let alone play the piano, as she loved to do in an earlier, happier time. The vivid descriptions of the hardships of the Dust Bowl underlie Billie Jo's burden of living through her guilt and injury. The story becomes one of overcoming those burdens, and Hesse's use of the images of the horror of the Dust Bowl and the poverty of the Great Depression years lend historic accuracy to Billie Jo's predicament.

Entertainment's Attempts to Lighten the Mood

Despite the pervading gloom from the high unemployment rate in the nation, the entertainment industry tried to brighten the mood with theater, film, and radio programs that allowed people to escape reality for a time. Whereas musicals such as *Gold Diggers* (1937), from American director Busby Berkeley, focused on the struggles of trying to make it in the work place, the upbeat lyrics and rhythms of the songs let audiences leave the theater with some optimism. Reflecting a belief in the power of benevolence, Frank Capra's *Mr. Deeds Goes to Town* (1936) has Gary Cooper playing a title character who resists greed as he helps the unemployed and destitute by sharing his inherited wealth. This was a scenario that many hoped could really occur. Escapism in movies like Capra's *Lost Horizon* (1937) also boosted morale with its tale of a utopia hidden among the peaks of the Himalayas.

Escape to Magic

The longest lasting success story in the entertainment industry from this era, however, goes to Walt Disney's creation of Mickey Mouse and the concept of using animated film in both movie shorts and in full-length features. Disney had begun making silent, short clips in the late 1920s and by 1932 won a special Academy Award for having introduced the character of Mickey Mouse to the American public at a time when laughter and happy endings were deeply appreciated. In 1935, Disney even won a League of Nations award honoring his creation of Mickey.

Mickey's growth in popularity accompanied multiple changes in the presentation of his character. In 1929, in *Karnival Kid*, he talked for the first time saying "hot dogs, hot dogs" and by 1935 he conducted Rossini's "William Tell Overture" in Technicolor, wearing his signature white gloves. As the decade progressed, story lines for Mickey Mouse had him in various conflicts that PARODIED popular genres from westerns to detective "who-dunnits" to love triangles. In all, Mickey prevailed with innocence and humor.

For a while in the late 1930s, Disney's new character Donald Duck surpassed Mickey in popularity by showing an interesting twist to human nature. Whereas Mickey was always loved as the "good guy," audiences showed a new affinity for the mischievous Donald who was brash and a trouble maker. Donald's funny garbled speech and harassment of Mickey delighted people. For instance, his interruptions of Mickey's conducting the orchestra in *Band Concert* with his own playing of "Turkey in the Straw" was a highlight of the short's instant success. With the introduction of Donald's nephews—Huey, Dewey, and Louie—Donald Duck became Mickey's alter ego. This inimitable combination of opposite personalities gave Disney and his associates one of the real economic triumphs of the Depression.

By 1934, the Disney studio began work on a new project with the belief that even during an economic disaster, fresh creative ideas were essential. In 1937, Disney presented its first full-length animated feature, *Snow White and the Seven Dwarfs*, to wildly enthusiastic audiences. The story, based on a Grimm Brothers' fairy tale, had familiar themes—a vulnerable princess, evil stepmother/witch, handsome prince, and helpful forest creatures. However, Disney's animators, under Walt's direction, brought a magic to the screen that audiences in those bleak years found to be entrancing. Snow White and the Prince are eternally good while the Queen/Witch is evil incarnate.

The personalities of the Seven Dwarfs have no parallel in the original tale and were the product of weeks of studio research and work. Doc, Grumpy, Happy, Sneezy, Sleepy, Bashful, and Dopey took America by storm with their comedic antics and loveable reactions to the mysterious young woman in their house. They emerged as celebrities in the coming years in the form of dolls, collector figurines, and even quiz show questions based on their names and characteristics. The American Film Institute named *Snow White and the Seven Dwarfs*, an innovation of the Depression, as one of the best 100 films of all times.

Other Fantasies

Another great fantasy experience of the decade was Metro-Goldwyn-Mayer's *The Wizard of Oz,* which premiered in 1939. Based on L. Frank Baum's children's book, *The Wonderful Wizard of Oz* (1900), MGM created a visual PARABLE of American hopes and fears. For a nation that still suffered from disastrous unemployment, lost homes, and homeless encampments, having a heroine from a Kansas farm who destroyed two witches with the help of three accomplices representing wisdom, courage, and love was an uplifting and inspiring combination. Added to the SYMBOLISM was the Technicolor spectacle of the Land of Oz with its spiraling yellow brick road, trees that talked, an Emerald City, and flying monkeys. Audiences were ready for this escape to fantasy in which empowered characters make the impossible happen.

In addition to the escapism of fairy tales and fantasy, comedies and detective films also answered the public's need to lose itself in fiction. Some of the best of the escapist films of the period still seen on late-night TV or rented online, include the comedy *It Happened One Night* (1934*)*, the classic detective story *Hound of the Baskervilles* (1939*)*, and *The Thin Man* (1934), each one a combination of humor and sleuthing.

It Happened One Night, a classic "screwball" comedy with famous Holywood stars Clark Gable and Claudette Colbert, follows

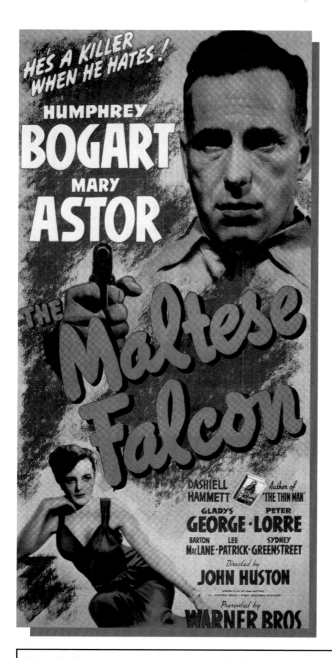

The Maltese Falcon by Dashiell Hammett
Also borne out of the hardships of the Depression was a hard-boiled detective genre. Dashiell Hammett's 1930 novel *The Maltese Falcon* became a classic film starring Humphrey Bogart as Sam Spade—the ultimate, cool private eye—and Spade became a model for Raymond Chandler's Philip Marlow, another protagonist of 1930's fiction. In those anxiety ridden times, these crime-fighting heroes were popular, in part, as counterpoints to despair.

a couple with multiple misunderstandings until they realize their true feelings for one another. It uses the rich-girl-and-poor-boy combination for a happy ending. *Hound of the Baskervilles,* the first Sherlock Holmes adventure from the Arthur Conan Doyle series, features the perfect English accents of actors Basil Rathbone and Nigel Bruce as they solve a mystery in a remote English manor. Holmes's superb confidence in solving every crime, at a time when confidence was low, satisfied audiences everywhere. Finally, *The Thin Man*, based on the Dashiel Hammett detective series, consisted of a fast-moving mystery with the popular stars William Powell and Myrna Loy as the wise-cracking married detectives whose dialogue kept audiences amused as the couple always tracked down the bad guys.

Going to the movies was an effective escape. Like popular fiction, it was a relatively inexpensive means of forgetting the pressures of the economic reality.

Another Escape

The top entertainer of the period in movies, radio, live performances, and print was Will Rogers (1879–1935). His dry, cowboy humor kept America smiling until his unexpected death in a plane crash in Alaska saddened the nation. Rogers was first a cowboy, performing amazing tricks with a lasso in Wild West shows and vaudeville, but he soon moved to films, making 50 silent movies and 21 "talkies." His one-liners and short observations on politics and life in general were folksy and down to earth but rich in irony. Rogers commented on current topics in "Daily Telegrams," syndicated in more than five thousand newspapers for more than a decade. During President Herbert Hoover's administration, in a March 20, 1931, column, he compared Wall Street bankers' maneuvers to the state of Nevada's requiring taxes on gambling: "If Wall Street paid tax on every game they run, we would get enough income to run the government on." He aligned himself with those who did not like or trust the bankers by poking fun at their "games." Shortly before the election of 1932, he came up with this joke: "The Republican says, 'Well, things could have been worse,' and the Democrat says, 'How?'" This punchline reflected the voting mood of the country and predicted the outcome of the presidential election.

After Roosevelt's win, Rogers describes one of FDR's speeches in a March 13, 1933, column as a "home run," because the president "did not use [the] big words that radio announcers and public speakers should leave in the dictionary." He added that it "is good Roosevelt made the dry topic of banking understandable because if the banks were liquid he would not have to speak at all." His audience understood and appreciated the understated, down-to-earth humor. His last "telegrams" before his plane crash were about the beauties of Alaska as he flew over the land with his friend Wiley Post. Rogers was so universally loved that newspapers across the country reported that people viewed his death as a personal loss.

Other Authors on the Great Depression

Although John Steinbeck is perhaps the author most associated with the Oklahoma Dust Bowl and the Great Depression, other writers also told heartbreaking stories about the country's hardships in these years. The Federal Writers' Project is credited with giving many a chance to eat, as well as write.

Edward Anderson

Edward Anderson (1905–1969) was one of the authors who lived the life he wrote about. He had been a journalist in Oklahoma, a deckhand, prizefighter, and even a fairly successful musician; however, by 1930, he was on the road, riding the trains as a hobo. His first novel, *Hungry Men* (1933), follows the travels of Arcel Stecker, an unemployed musician roaming the country by hopping on freight cars. He spends time in flophouses, rail cars, and court rooms always trying to find something to eat. The book was declared an outstanding example of the mood of the time as the reader experiences the protagonist's misery and loss of hope. Four years later, *Thieves Like Us* (1937) painted an even bleaker picture as three escaped convicts manage to pull off a string of successful robberies as they run through Texas and Oklahoma. However, the law catches up with them, and they are doomed to failure. Whereas Anderson's novels were almost forgotten for years, their stories of young men without jobs or purpose still resonate with the reality of the Great Depression.

Nathanael West, Horace McCoy, and Josephine Johnson

On the other hand, Nathanael West, born Nathan Weinstein (1903–1940), is one of the best known of the Great Depression writers, partly because his novels were adapted to film. West reveals the secrets and urban despair of that era in his *Day of the Locust* (1939), set in the early days of Hollywood. He describes the contrast between those on the edge of success and those at its center. West uses vivid, unusual images to describe Hollywood in contrast to the poverty of most of the country. The novel ends in violence with a mob rioting outside a movie premiere.

Earlier, in 1933, in *Miss Lonelyhearts*, West focused on the emotional breakdown of a young man who writes an advice column for a New York paper. The forlorn letters he receives convey the true pathos of the era. The letters come from a population who is so alienated and in pain that Miss Lonelyhearts' unexpected death is almost a blessing. Both novels express the dark emotions of the era.

Like West, Horace McCoy (1897–1955) discovered inspiration in southern California, finding his ideas for his novel *They Shoot Horses, Don't They* (1935), also adapted for film, after working as a bouncer on the Santa Monica pier by the Pacific Ocean. His characters are desperate for the free food, bed, and the $1,000 prize they will receive if they win a dance marathon. The details of the participants' humiliation and injuries make death seem almost preferable. The book was better received in Europe than in the United States, where its bleak setting was perhaps too familiar. In a similar vein of desperation, Henry Roth (1906–1995) describes the squalid city environment of a New York Jewish ghetto in *Call It Sleep* (1934) and the anxieties that exist in such a setting. He uses stream-of-consciousness technique to reveal the perceptions of a young boy, the son of IMMIGRANT parents, and stark realism to describe the poverty of that section of the city.

Josephine W. Johnson (1910–1990) won a Pulitzer Prize for her novel *Now in November* (1934). Set in a midwestern town, some critics find these descriptions of the Dust Bowl even more vivid than those in the better-known *Grapes of Wrath*. The Hardmarne family barely survives the drought, but it is the tension between the three daughters and their father that really holds the reader's attention. The narrator's tone illustrates a compelling sense of both hope and despair. *Jordanstown* (1937), also set in the Midwest, follows a small town journalist who tries to answer the issues of the era in his columns.

Appointment in Samarra

John O'Hara's (1905–1970) first novel *Appointment in Samarra* (1936) focuses on Julian English, whose elitist, arrogant behavior certainly makes him an unsympathetic protagonist for a period of such obvious disparity in wealth. Ironically, O'Hara himself has been described as obsessed with status. Critic Brendan Gill, who was an associate at the literary magazine *The New Yorker*, has said that he admired O'Hara's work but found him difficult to be with. The death of O'Hara's father had prevented him from attending the college of his choice, Yale, and O'Hara's avowed disappointment may have been the catalyst for the cynicism and social criticism found in his stories and novels. In addition to novels and screenplays, O'Hara was a war correspondent during World War II (1941–1945) and later wrote numerous short stories for *The New Yorker*. He won the National Book Award in 1955 for his novel, *Ten North Frederick*.

In *Appointment in Samarra,* English's deliberate ignorance of how his actions affect others establishes him as almost a PARODY of those unfazed by the economic hardships of the 1930s. English owns a Cadillac dealership (the ultimate status symbol in his small city of Gibbsville) belongs to the local country club, and lives on the street known for being the best address. His wife Caroline is the daughter of one of the city's leaders. English takes all these advantages for granted and then proceeds to destroy himself. He attempts to seduce other women, drinks himself to oblivion, and deliberately throws a drink on Harry Reilly to whom he and others owe money. His wife Caroline tries to explain the reality of his behavior:

> . . . but I don't have to tell you there's a Depression in this country, and Harry Reilly's practically the only man around with any money.

English is rude to the servants in his home and even antagonizes the local mobster who in the past has not only bought cars from English's dealership but also recommended the company to others. O'Hara precedes all this with a story about a man who tries to flee Death only to find that in fleeing he has gone directly to Death's location. With that introduction, it is no surprise that English thinks he is a failure and finds suicide the only solution. O'Hara's veiled disapproval of the status-seeking English parallels much of the country's attitude toward those who were oblivious to the general economic pain of the nation.

The Big Money

An awareness of the great economic gaps in this country is also the subject of *The Big Money* (1936) by John Dos Passos. This is the last book in his *U.S.A.* trilogy which covers the first third of the twentieth century. Although Dos Passos's work is fiction, as he follows several characters in *The Big Money* from the end of WWI (1914–1918) through the beginning of the Great Depression, he weaves in biographical sketches, personal perspective, newspaper headlines, and song lyrics among the stories of his fictional characters. For example, his character Charley Anderson first appears in *The 42nd Parallel* as a youth from North Dakota, as a soldier in *1919*, and finally as a failure and a drunk at the end of *The Big Money*. Anderson's steady decline parallels what Dos Passos observed in the United States in the 1930s.

Dos Passos also incorporates his own perspective. In a stream-of-consciousness style, he vehemently sides with the nation's workers, including the immigrants and their children, who were often viewed with deep suspicion:

> . . . in the law's office we stand against the wall the law is a big man with eyes angry in a big pumpkinface who sits and stares at us meddling foreigners through the door the deputies crane with their guns they stand guard at the mines they blockade the miners' soupkitchens they've cut off the road up the valley . . . sits easy a his desk his back is covered he feels strong behind him he feels the prosecutingattorney the judge an owner himself the political boss the mine superintendent the board of directors the president of the utility the manipulator of the holding company.

In addition, Dos Passos juxtaposes headlines from the newspaper *The New York World* with excerpts from song lyrics. In "Newsreel LXVIII," he exposes the hypocrisy of the times:

> REAL VALUES UNHARMED
> *While we slave for the bosses*
> *Our children scream an' cry*
> *But when we draw our money*
> *Our grocery bills to pay*
> PRESIDENT SEES PROSPERITY NEAR
> *Not a cent to spend for clothing*
> *Not a cent to layway*

Finally, Dos Passos includes short, unorthodox biographies of real people, including Thomas Edison and publisher William Randolph Hearst. He began Hearst's biography with these lines:

> Mrs. Hearst's son was born in sixtythree. Nothing too good for the only son . . . . grew up solemneyed and selfwilled among servants and hired men, factotum, overseers, hangerson, old pensioners, his grandparents spoiled him; he always did everything he wanted. Mrs. Hearst's boy must have everything of the best.

He closes the biography with these words:

Jail the reds, praising the comforts of Baden-Baden under the blood and bludgeon rule of Handsome Adolph (Hearst's own loved invention, the lowest common denominator come to power out of the rot of democracy) complaining about the California incometax shrilling about the dangers of thought in the colleges. Deport; jail.

Dos Passos became perhaps more questioning of his liberal values as he aged, but during the writing of his famous trilogy, especially *The Big Money,* his own elitist background made him all the more aware of the dire economic disparities in the country and the brutality that often accompanied those desperate circumstances. In the closing section, he contrasts the character Vag's miserable hitchhike across the land with the comforts of those who are flying above him.

These six authors were deeply influenced by and are remembered for their reactions to these hard years. Their vivid stories reveal an era in which people struggled through natural disasters, economic failure, and personal hardship.

In the decade from 1929 to 1939, the Great Depression inspired multiple authors to record the emotions and actions of those affected. When lives are unexpectedly changed and challenged, writers are inspired to share universal experiences and to understand more clearly the human spirit.

Timeline

Science, Technology, and the Arts	Literature	History
1909 First mass production line for automobiles **1910** Stravinsky *Firebird Suite* **1911** Berlin *Alexander's Ragtime Band* **1912** **1913** Armory Show of modern art in New York City Duchamp *Nude Descending a Staircase* Stravinsky *The Rite of Spring* **1914** Gas mask invented **1915** D. W. Griffith *Intolerance* Einstein's general theory of relativity Pyrex invented **1916** First radio tuner invented **1917** George M. Cohan, *Over There* **1918** **1919** Invention of the arc welder **1920** Earle Dickson invents the Band-Aid	Stein *Three Lives* Dreiser *Jennie Gerhardt* Mann *Death in Venice* Johnson *Autobiography of an Ex-Colored Man* Cather *O Pioneers!* Kafka *The Metamorphosis* Lawrence *Sons and Lovers* Frost *North of Boston* Joyce *A Portrait of the Artist as a Young Man* Frost *Mountain Interval* Sandburg *Chicago Poems* Lardner *You Know Me Al* Eliot *Prufrock and Other Observations* Cather *My Ántonia* Anderson *Winesburg, Ohio* Colette *Cheri* Fitzgerald *This Side of Paradise* Lawrence *Women in Love* Lewis *Main Street* O'Neill *The Emperor Jones* Pound *Hugh Selwyn Mauberly* Dos Passos *Three Soldiers* Moore *Poems*	NAACP founded by W. E. B. Du Bois and others US population: 91,972,266 Pres. Wilson inaugurated Start of World War I in Europe Ku Klux Klan reborn Easter Uprising in Ireland for home rule US enters World War I Russian Revolution Volstead Act prohibits liquor (18th Amendment to US Constitution.) Treaty of Versailles ends WWI Civil War in Ireland American women given the vote League of Nations first meets

Science, Technology, and the Arts	Literature	History
1921	O'Neill *Anna Christie* Eliot *The Waste Land*	
1922 Insulin invented by Sir Frederick Grant Banting	Joyce *Ulysses* Fitzgerald *The Beautiful and Damned* Lewis *Babbitt* McKay *Harlem Shadows* Frost *New Hampshire*	U.S.S.R. is formed
1923 Garret A. Morgan invents the traffic signal	Kafka *The Trial* Stevens *Harmonium* Toomer *Cane* Kafka *The Castle*	Teapot Dome scandal
1924	Lardner *How to Write Short Stories* O'Neill *Desire Under the Elms*	
1925 *The New Yorker* magazine started by Harold Ross Charlie Chaplin stars in *The Gold Rush* Television developed by John Logie Baird	Dos Passos *Manhattan Transfer* Dreiser *An American Tragedy* Fitzgerald *The Great Gatsby* Hemingway *In Our Time* Lewis *Arrowsmith* Pound starts writing the *Cantos* Faulkner *Soldier's Pay*	Scopes Monkey trial
1926 Robert H. Goddard develops liquid fueled rockets	Hemingway *The Sun Also Rises* Hughes *Weary Blues* Van Vechten *Nigger Heaven*	President Coolidge sends marines to Nicaragua
1927 Iron lung first made	Hemingway *Men Without Women* Lewis *Elmer Gantry* McKay *Return to Harlem*	Babe Ruth hits 60 home runs Lindbergh flies NY-Paris Collapse of German economy
1928 Alexander Fleming discovers penicillin	O'Neill *Strange Interlude*	First Mickey Mouse cartoon
1929	Faulkner *The Sound and the Fury* Hemingway *A Farewell to Arms* Lewis *Dodsworth* Wolfe *Look Homeward, Angel*	Stock market collapses in October
1930 Invention of Scotch tape Clarence Birdseye invents frozen foods	Sinclair Lewis receives Nobel Prize for literature Dos Passos *The 42nd Parallel*	Gandhi begins campaign of Civil Disobedience in India

Science, Technology, and the Arts	Literature	History
1931 Dalí *The Persistence of Memory* Max Knott and Ernest Ruska invent the electron microscope Harold Edgerton invents stop-action photography	Eliot *Ash Wednesday* Faulkner *As I Lay Dying* Guthrie "Travelin' Hard"	
1932 First parking meter made by Charles C. McGee **1933** **1934**	Dos Passos *1919* Faulkner *Light in August* Anderson *Hungry Men* Stein *The Autobiography of Alice B. Toklas* West *Miss Lonelyhearts* Fitzgerald *Tender Is the Night* Johnson *Now in November* Roth *Call It Sleep* Frost *A Further Range* Hemingway *The Green Hills of Africa*	Wisconsin milk strike Franklin Roosevelt inaugurated Hitler chancellor of Germany Prohibition ends in US
1935 Dupont Labs develop nylon **1936** Eugene O'Neill awarded Nobel Prize for literature	McCoy *They Shoot Horses, Don't They?* Steinbeck *Tortilla Flat* Eliot *Collected Poems* Faulkner *Absalom, Absalom!* Mitchell *Gone With the Wind* Steinbeck *In Dubious Battle* Hemingway *To Have and Have Not*	First Dust Bowl storms Start of Spanish Civil War
1937 Picasso *Guernica* Chester Carlson develops the photocopier	Anderson *Thieves Like Us* Johnson *Jordanstown* Hurston *Their Eyes Were Watching God*	Abraham Lincoln Brigade organizes in Spain Republic Steel massacre
1938 First ball point pen made by Ladislo Biro	Steinbeck *Of Mice and Men* Cummings *Collected Poems* Hemingway *The Fifth Column and the First Forty-Nine Stories* Sartre *Nausea*	Germany annexes Austria
1939 Sikorsky invents the helicopter Electron microscope developed New York World's Fair	Wilder *Our Town* Joyce *Finnegans Wake* Steinbeck *The Grapes of Wrath*	Franco captures Barcelona Germany annexes Czechoslovakia
1940 Penicillin developed	West *The Day of the Locust* Guthrie "Tom Joad" Auden *Another Time*	Russia invades Poland

Science, Technology, and the Arts	Literature	History
1940	Hemingway *For Whom the Bell Tolls* McCullers *The Heart is a Lonely Hunter* Wright *Native Son*	
1941	Fitzgerald *The Last Tycoon* (posthumous) McCullers *Reflections in a Golden Eye* Eliot *Four Quartets*	Japanese attack Pearl Harbor US enters World War II
1942 John Atanasoff and Clifford Berry make the first electronic digital computer	Wright *Black Boy*	Battle of Midway; end of Japanese expansion
1943		Italy surrenders
1944		D Day in Europe
1945 Copeland *Appalachian Spring*		Germany surrenders Nuclear bombs dropped on Japan
1946	Hersey *Hiroshima*	Japan surrenders

Glossary of Terms

allusion a reference, usually an unexplained one, as when T. S. Eliot incorporates sections of Shakespeare's *Antony and Cleopatra* in *The Waste Land* or when Faulkner titles his 1936 novel *Absalom, Absalom!,* referring to the book of II Samuel and King David's son

Armory Show celebrated exhibition of Modern Art held in New York in 1913, bringing the work of the radical avant-garde (Matisse, Picasso, Duchamp, etc.) to the American public for the first time

aphorism a pithy statement of a truth or concept

bootlegger a seller of illegal liquor during Prohibition (1919–1933). The origin of the term is obscure.

cause célèbre French for "a celebrated case," or a controversial event that involves legal proceedings and attracts a number of important people to one side or the other, such as the trial of the Scottsboro boys or the Scopes Monkey trial, about the teaching of evolution (1925)

communism the dictatorship of the ordinary people for the sake of the ordinary people. Socialism does not advocate such a dictatorship. Vladimir Lenin thought socialism was the first step toward Communism.

Depression see "Great Depression"

entrepreneur a businessperson; one who organizes, takes risks with, and promotes a venture—such as publishing a book, opening a nightclub, establishing a store, or starting a "line" of products

Dust Bowl during the 1930s, the ecological and economic area in which naturally occurring drought and the human removal of the topsoil brought ruin to the farms of the Midwest and its people. Large farms, which had been plowed strictly to grow wheat, contributed to the loss of vegetation, allowing the topsoil, during periods of drought, to drift and disappear in massive wind storms. Diversified farm practices and soil conservation eventually repaired most of the damage, but for more than a decade, many farmers in the Great Plains had to abandon their farms.

eros or erotic concerned with love, with self-preservation, and therefore with the urge to reproduce—hence allied to sex. One of the two principal drives in Freud's conceptualizing of personality, the other being thanatos, the death urge. Erotic urges can be expressed symbolically as well as directly.

expressionism the objectification of interior, emotional, and psychological states through dramatic devices

Federal Writers' Project established in 1935 as part of the larger federal assistance program known as the Work Progress Administration (WPA), a government program to provide work for the unemployed during the Great Depression. It was aimed at helping white-collar workers and is credited with providing money for research projects, theater groups, geologists, writers, and photographers. Many famous writers were helped by this program, including Nobel Prize winners Saul Bellow and John Steinbeck.

Freudian deriving from the ideas of Sigmund Freud, Viennese psychologist who explained human behavior in terms of the drives toward sex and death (eros and thanatos); often erroneously used as a substitute for "sexual." Freud felt that males as they matured went through an Oedipal phase of wanting to sleep with their mothers and kill their fathers; girls went through an Electra phase of desiring their fathers and disliking their mothers. His ideas influenced many thinkers, artists, and writers.

Gothic novel a long sensational story full of supernatural occurrences set against a romantic backdrop, usually with decaying buildings, and an atmosphere of menace and death

Great Depression period in the United States from 1929 to World War II characterized by lack of employment opportunities, poverty, and labor unrest

Hemingway myth in the 1930s, the writer Ernest Hemingway became a hero, a figure of legend, to many Americans. They saw his devotion to his craft (writing), his enthusiasm for physical pleasure in sports and in living well, as an answer to the purposelessness of the age

Holocaust the mass extermination of Jews and other groups such as Gypsies carried out by the Nazis during World War II; the mass extermination of any group of people

Hoovervilles homes to the unemployed, ranging from simple encampments by highways or railroads to shantytowns with spontaneous forms of government. These were named in ironic honor of President Herbert Hoover, who was perceived by many to have done little to help the 25% of the nation who were unemployed during the Great Depression.

iambic one unstressed accent followed by a stressed one. Most English poetry and most English speech is more or less iambic: The MAN could NOT conTROL the TRUCK, and so it SWERVed and KILLed a CAT.

iconoclast literally "idol breaker" who refuses established values, or someone who breaks with venerated practices or ideals

ideographs pictures that make up writing in Chinese, Japanese, and other Asian languages. Ezra Pound uses ideographs in his *Cantos.*

imagism poetic practice started by Ezra Pound and followed by William Carlos Williams and others. It supported the direct presentation of a sight, sound, smell, taste, or feel without any embellishment

Jazz Age period following World War I (1914–1918) in the United States characterized by listening to jazz music, seeking entertainment, usually with the understanding that life offered no higher, transcendent values; phrase coined by F. Scott Fitzgerald

lost generation men and women in their twenties and thirties who had lived through the traumatic event of World War I and felt themselves bereft of faith in civilization and distrustful of all ideals

lyricism usual mode of poetry and often of prose: an intense outpouring of emotion, often of a sensual character. The word derives from "lyre," an ancient Greek instrument that was the precursor of the guitar.

margin an investor's equity in securities bought with credit specifically obtained to buy those securities. Many investors in the United States who had purchased stocks on margin during the

1920s lost everything when the value of those stocks dropped precipitously in 1929.

mecca destination for pilgrims in the Islamic world (capitalized); by extension any center of activity for people engaged in the pursuit of a common goal

mechanization, myth of the machine fear after World War I that humanity had lost control of itself and that machines had replaced people as the essential actors in the important activities of living

mimetic the imitation of aspects of reality in literature and art

naturalism literary practice of presenting life as it is lived with no moralizing or editorial interference on the part of the author

novella work of fiction of intermediate length between a short story and a novel

picaresque from the Spanish for rogue or rascal, a style of novel, loosely plotted, that tells the story or series of adventures of a person of low social status

primitivism a feeling that basic, uncivilized instinctual behavior is more validated because so-called civilized social activities are contaminated by things such as oppression, racism, and deadening convention

Prohibition a period in the United States (1919–1933) during which the sale of liquor (alcohol) was forbidden. The Volstead Act of 1919 amended the Constitution to enact this law, which was not repealed until Franklin D. Roosevelt became president.

proselytize to induce someone to convert to a faith or idea

realism the literary term that denotes reliance on fact or actuality in writing as opposed to that which idealizes or fantasizes; *See also* **literary realism**

salon drawing room or parlor, usually populated by people of intellectual, cultural, or social distinction, who gather for the civilized exchange of views

sharecroppers also known as tenant farmers or subsistence farmers, those who pay rent for farmland by giving to the landowner a share of the crops raised. Once common in the South for former slaves after the Civil War (1861–1865) and for those had little cash. Because there was no regulation of the amount required, landowners were known to change terms and take advantage of uneducated tenants, including charging high interest rates. This group endured severe hardship during the Great Depression.

socialist an adherent of a social system in which all the workers own all the property and work for the common good

squib a short, humorous, piece of writing

stream of consciousness a literary practice that attempts to depict the mental and emotional reactions of characters to external events, rather than the events themselves, through the practice of reproducing the unedited, continuous sequence of thoughts that run through a person's head, most usually without punctuation or literary interference

surrealism an artistic practice that assembles familiar matter in new ways, with new properties, as exemplified in the paintings of Salvador Dalí or Réné Magritte. Literally it means "beyond" realism. The term was coined by the French surrealist poet André Breton in 1924.

syllabics in poetry the practice of basing a line on the number of syllables in it, as opposed to the number of rhythmic feet (e.g., three iambs, or iambic tetrameter)

thanatos the urge toward death; a basic impulse toward death considered by Sigmund Freud as the opposite of eros, the life instinct

trochaic tetrameter a verse line of four feet, with each foot comprised of a stressed syllable followed by an unstressed syllable. This line from William Blake is in trochaic tetrameter: "Tyger, tyger, burning bright."

trope figure of speech

vernacular everyday speech of a people as opposed to specifically literary language

Works Progress Administration (WPA) established in 1935 by President Franklin D. Roosevelt in response to the 25% unemployment in 1933 when he took office during the Great Depression. This government agency provided work to unskilled laborers at about $25 dollars a month and to white-collar workers at about $80 per month. Projects ranged from highway and public building construction to field research for artists and photographers. The program was both praised and criticized.

World War I from 1914 to 1918, took place mainly in Europe, with the United States entering in 1918. In the first years, Germany, Austria-Hungary, and Turkey (the Central Powers) were allied against Russia, France, Italy, and Great Britain (the Allies). Grueling trench warfare, poison gas, and airplanes were first used in this conflict. Although the harsh reparations or penalties against the defeated nations helped perpetrate Adolf Hitler's rise to power in Germany, the general economic and political instability of the time resulted also in Italy's Fascist government as well as Russia's revolution and its move toward communism.

World War II An international conflict that began in 1939 with the German invasion of Poland and ended in 1945 with the detonation of the first nuclear bomb in Hiroshima, Japan. U.S. involvement began in 1941, after the Japanese bombed Pearl Harbor in Hawaii. The principal opponents were the Axis powers—Germany, Italy, and Japan—and the Allies—principally France, Great Britain, the United States, and the Soviet Union.

zeppelin A rigid airship consisting of a covered frame supported by internal gas cells. Derived from the name of its inventor, Ferdinand Graf von Zeppelin (1838–1917).

Biographical Glossary

Breton, André (1896–1966) Born in the Department of Orne, in France, Breton was a medical student and worked in psychiatric units of French hospitals in World War I. After the war, in Paris, he became interested in alternative forms of expression. Influenced by Freud, he wrote frequently for the magazine *Littérature.* Breton coined the term *surrealisme* in 1924. He wrote a novel and published three influential manifestos of surrealist thought. An antirationalist, Breton's poetry was influenced by Arthur Rimbaud (1854–1891) and Paul Valéry (1871–1945).

Cullen, Countee (1903–1946) Born Countee Porter in Louisville, Kentucky, and raised by his grandmother, he moved to New York at the age of fourteen and adopted the name of his foster parents. In 1925 at New York University he won a poetry prize and published his first collection, *Color,* the same year. More prizes and a second volume, *Copper Sun* (1927), followed. He was briefly married to W. E. B. Du Bois's daughter Yolande. In 1934 he began teaching high school—English and French—in New York, where essayist and novelist James Baldwin was one of his students. His collected poems, *On Thee I Stand,* appeared one year before his death.

Cummings, E. E. (1894–1962) Cummings's father was a Unitarian minister. Like Du Bois and Eliot, he attended Harvard and gave the 1915 senior commencement address on "the new art," that is, modernism in literature, painting (a lifelong interest; Cummings was a talented painter as well as a poet), and music. A friend of John Dos Passos, he drove an ambulance in World War I and was wrongly detained on suspicion of being a spy, an experience that he used in his narrative *The Enormous Room* (1922). His first collection, *Tulips and Chimneys,* appeared in 1923, followed by *XLI Poems* (1925). *ViVa* came out in 1931. He became the common-law husband of the model Marion Morehouse in 1933. *No Thanks* (1935) and several editions of his collected work followed, together with four volumes of poems, many with numerical titles: *50 Poems* (1940), *1 × 1* (1945), *XIAPE* (1950), and *95 Poems* (1958).

Dalí, Salvador (1904–1989) Born in Catalonia, Spain, Dalí began painting in Madrid at the age of thirteen, rapidly absorbing the schools of cubism and futurism then fashionable. In 1929 he joined the surrealist movement and his ability to promote himself quickly made Dalí the best-known painter of the movement. He deliberately cultivated the bizarre in his art and his life. Later, he worked in a number of other media, such as jewelry, motion pictures, and theatrical design. In his old age Dalí became something of a recluse, although he continued to repeat images he favored in the 1930s, sometimes interweaving portraits of his wife, Gala, and often increasing the sexual content of his paintings.

Dos Passos, John (1896–1970) The illegitimate son of a New York lawyer, John Dos Passos spent his earliest years traveling with his mother in Europe and spoke French before he knew English. After education at Choate and Harvard, he served as an ambulance driver in World War I. He did not believe in the war and formed a coterie of literary friends, some of whom he had met at Harvard—e.e. Cummings, Robert Hillyer, and Ernest Hemingway. In 1921 he published *Three Soldiers.* He exhibited his paintings in New York and there worked on *Manhattan Transfer,* published to acclaim. Traveling to Mexico but keeping New York as a base, Dos Passos published the three volumes of *U.S.A.* in 1927–1936. He changed from Communist to Socialist to "middle class liberal." He met and in 1929 eventually married Katy Smith, a friend of Hemingway's. Throughout his life, Dos Passos suffered from rheumatic fever. He worked on a film about Spain with Hemingway. Katy died in an automobile accident in 1947; in the same accident Dos Passos lost his right eye. Dos Passos died of congestive heart failure in Baltimore, aged 74.

Du Bois, W[illiam] E[dward] B[urkhardt] (1868–1963) Born in Great Barrington, Massachusetts, Du Bois studied philosophy at Harvard, like T.S. Eliot. At the Paris Exposition of 1900, he organized an exhibition on black economic progress. *The Souls of Black Folk,* essays, appeared three years later. After a biography of John Brown and a novel, he helped found the National Association for the Advancement of Colored People (NAACP) in 1909 and edited its magazine, *The Crisis,* until 1934. Du Bois traveled extensively throughout Russia and Africa, publishing fiction, essays, and an autobiography, *Dusk of Dawn* (1934). Du Bois suffered from the pandemic distrust of social radicals in the 1950s. He settled in Ghana shortly before his death at age 95.

Eliot, T[homas] S[tearns] (1888–1965) Born in St. Louis in 1888, Eliot like Ezra Pound studied romance and classical languages as a young man. He returned to Harvard to pursue studies in philosophy in the same year as he composed "The Love Song of J. Alfred Prufrock." In 1915 he married a mentally distressed young woman, which probably contributed to his own mental unease. He worked as a banker even while publishing in *Poetry* and after his first book of verse had appeared. He continued to publish poetry and criticism while suffering a breakdown in 1921, when he composed *The Waste Land.* In 1922 he founded *The Criterion* magazine. In 1925 he joined the publishing firm of Faber and Faber and published *The Hollow Men.* Two years later Eliot became a British citizen and joined the Anglican Church. Separated from his wife in 1932, he wrote verse dramas throughout the 1930s. His last book of poetry, *Four Quartets,* appeared in 1942, six years before he won the Nobel Prize and the English Order of Merit.

Faulkner, William (1897–1962) Although Faulkner was raised in a bourgeois southern family, with a history of violence as well as some literary production, his earliest influence was his mammy Caroline Barr, the black dedicatee of *The Hamlet* (1940), who early on took care of Faulkner and his siblings, telling them stories and walking in the woods. While working in his father's livery stable and courting his future wife Estelle Oldham, Faulkner met Phil Stone, a law student, who introduced him to literature. Faulkner discovered his voice when he started writing fiction under the guidance of Sherwood Anderson. He published five monumental works of modernism and southern life: *The Sound and the Fury* (1929), *As I Lay Dying* (1930), *Sanctuary* (1931), *Light in August* (1932), and *Absalom, Absalom!* (1936). He worked in Hollywood to earn money. The publication in the 1940s of *The Portable Faulkner* consolidated his reputation. Adored by French intellectuals, Faulkner won the Nobel Prize in 1949, stating magnificently, "I believe that man will not merely endure: he will prevail." He alternated between periods of working and drinking, and died of a heart attack in Mississippi in 1962.

Fitzgerald, F. Scott (1896–1940) "The poet of the Jazz Age," seen today as the embodiment of the roaring 1920s, Fitzgerald was raised in St. Paul, Minnesota, and in his teens fell in love with a society belle from Lake Forest, Illinois. He attended Princeton University where he wrote theatricals and partied, leaving before he completed his degree. In 1918, while stationed in the army in Alabama, he met Zelda Sayre, a beautiful, unstable young woman. This romance and the previous he wrote into his first successful novel, *This Side of Paradise,* a commercial success in 1920. The rest of his life he spent as a writer of popular magazine fiction for *The Saturday Evening Post* as well as the author of increasingly affecting, serious novels. His masterpiece, *The Great Gatsby* (1925), was followed by *Tender Is the Night* (1934) as well as memorable short stories: "May Day," "The Diamond as Big as the Ritz," "The Rich Boy," and "Babylon Revisited." Alcoholic and temperamental, he spent his last year paying off debts incurred by high living. He was working in Hollywood and writing a novel about the movie business when he died of heart attack.

Freud, Sigmund (1856–1939) Born into a comfortable middle-class Jewish family, Freud's family relocated to Vienna, the city with which he is permanently identified. In 1873 he began studies in medicine in that city. More interested in science than in practicing medicine, he started out as a neurologist. His association with the physiologist Josef Breuer led him to research what Breuer called a "talking cure." In 1900 his researches in this area led him to publish his most influential book *The Interpretation of Dreams,* a study of the unconscious mind. Throughout his career he continued to reformulate and refine his investigations in this area, producing study after study, devoted to medical and psychological subjects ("Character and Anal Eroticism" [1908]), while others explored the lives of artists (*Leonardo da Vinci and a Memory of his Childhood* [1910]), religion (*The Future of an Illusion* [1927]), or dealt with civilization as a whole (*Civilization and Its Discontents* [1930]). Suffering from cancer, he was persecuted by the Nazis. Forced into exile in 1938, he died in England the following year.

Frost, Robert (1874–1963) Although most closely identified with New England, Frost was born in San Francisco and moved to the East when young. A brilliant though erratic student, he spent only a brief time at Dartmouth before trying his hand at farming, teaching, and writing stories and poetry. A trip to England, where he met Ezra Pound and European poets, including Yeats and Edward Thomas, resulted in the publication of his first two books, *A Boy's Will* (1914) and *North of Boston* (1915). These became successful in America. He relocated to northern New England (New Hampshire and then Vermont) and continued writing and lecturing for the next 60 years, producing *New Hampshire* (1923), *West Running Brook* (1928), *A Further Range* (1936), *A Witness Tree* (1942), *Steeple Bush* (1947), and *In the Clearing* (1962). Venerated and honored in his last decades, he read a poem at the inauguration of President John F. Kennedy (1960).

Hemingway, Ernest (1899–1961) Born in Oak Park, Illinois, to a religious mother and a father who was a doctor and who would, in 1927, commit suicide, Hemingway early on loved outdoor life, hunting, and fishing. He served in the Italian army in World War I, where in 1918 he was wounded. While in Italy, Hemingway fell in love with a nurse, who would later serve as a model for Catherine Barkley in *A Farewell to Arms.* He associated with the expatriates in Paris in the early 1920s, publishing two small books before his first New York publication, *In Our Time* (1925), a group of related stories. A small satire followed and was succeeded by his first great success, *The Sun Also Rises* (1926), the novel of the "lost generation." Famous for his rugged, athletic life as well as his impeccable prose style, Hemingway published *A Farewell to Arms* (1929), a study of bullfighting, *Death in the Afternoon* (1932), and many influential short stories. Hemingway fought in the Spanish Civil War, an experience that resulted in *For Whom the Bell Tolls* (1940). His later work declined in quality. Ill and depressed, he shot himself in his home in Ketchum, Idaho, in 1961.

Guthrie, Woodrow (Woody) (1912–1967) Singer, songwriter, and writer. Woody Guthrie began his life in Oklahoma with family tragedies: his sister's death, his mother's debilitating illness, and financial ruin. As a result, he took to the road, ending up in Texas, where he married Mary Jennings, the sister of a musician friend with whom he started a musical career. However, as the 1935 Dust Bowl made it impossible to earn a living, Woody took to the road again, this time ending up in California. He rode the rails, hitchhiked, walked and earned his food by singing in saloons and even painting signs. He lived the life that he later sang about when he was hired by the radio station KFVD in Los Angeles, providing social commentary about the desperate plight of his fellow Okies. His success moved him to New York, where he continued to take the side of the underdog, singing and playing the guitar with Pete Seeger and a group that later became known as the Weavers. He also spent some time in Oregon working on a film project for the government, after which he hitchhiked back to New York, leaving his first wife in Texas. Returning to his ideas of social activism, Guthrie lived in Coney Island with his new wife, Marjorie, and their four children. During World War II, he served in the Merchant Marines and the Army, writing songs inspired by his hatred of Fascism and his belief in social justice. He also collected his memories from the Dust Bowl years and published

them as a novel, *Bound for Glory* (1943). By the late 1940s, Huntington disease, a degenerative genetic disorder, began to affect his mental health, however, and he became unpredictable in his actions. It was during this time that he moved to California, married his third wife, and became part of Joseph McCarthy's blacklist of "accused communists," along with many other public and celebrity figures who were known for their social activism. A month after Woody died, his son Arlo Guthrie released "Alice's Restaurant," which became the hugely popular anti-war song for the next generation. Woody wrote numerous unpublished works, two novels, and almost 3,000 lyrics, including the beloved–"This Land Is Your Land."

Hersey, John (1914–1993) War correspondent and novelist. As a journalist born in China, Hersey's interest in Asia led him to interview and write about the results of the World War II Hiroshima bombing within a year of its occurrence. His matter-of-fact tone, accurate details, and vivid narrative style led to his immediate recognition. *Hiroshima* was published in the August 13, 1946, issue of *The New Yorker*, with subsequent publication in book form. Hersey had served on both fronts during the war as a correspondent, but after the publication of *Hiroshima,* he returned to writing fiction. He taught writing at Yale University and in the 1970s tried to explain the Civil Rights and antiwar movements to students and alumni. He published 18 works besides *Hiroshima*, most of them fiction because he said that it is the emotions of people that count. Throughout his life, he also wrote numerous articles on current issues such as education and race relations.

Hughes, Langston (1902–1967) After Hughes's father abandoned his family in Missouri, Hughes grew up in Lawrence, Kansas, with his grandmother. After visiting Mexico and attending Columbia University for a short while, Hughes worked at various odd jobs and continued traveling. He was friends with Countee Cullen and corresponded with Alain Locke. He was "discovered" when poet Vachel Lindsay, who was staying at a hotel where Hughes was a busboy, read some of his poems in public. *The Weary Blues* (1926), his first collection, resulted, to be followed by *Fine Clothes to the Jew* (1927), and a novel. Eventually, after teaching in Atlanta, Hughes bought a property in Harlem. More collections of poems followed, all while Hughes was traveling in Africa and Europe. His final collections were *Ask Your Mama* (1961) and *The Panther and the Lash* (1967).

Hurston, Zora Neale (1891–1960) Although Hurston was born in Alabama, her family moved to central Florida in 1894. She later went to Howard

University, where she studied while working as a manicurist. New York, however, drew her with its circle of writers and artists, and in 1925 she went there and began writing and publishing fiction, associating with Countee Cullen, Langston Hughes, Fannie Hurst, and Carl Van Vechten and becoming a part of the Harlem Renaissance. A short marriage to a medical student slowed down but did not impede her research in African American folklore, which eventually resulted in the publication of *Mules and Men* (1935). While continuing research in Haiti, she wrote *Their Eyes Were Watching God* in 1936, which was published the next year to good reviews. She joined the Federal Writers' Project in Florida while working on her next novel, *Moses, Man of the Mountain* (1939). A notably independent woman, Hurston continued to work on a variety of projects and produced numerous magazine articles, eventually publishing her last novel, *Seraph on the Suwanee* (1948), which was also positively received. After legal troubles, she returned to central Florida in the mid-1950s, working as a substitute teacher before dying in poverty and obscurity from heart disease.

Joyce, James (1882–1941) Irish writer. James Joyce's works have had a great impact on later writers with their interior monologues, "stream of consciousness" technique, and symbolic parallels from mythology and history. His semi-autobiographical novel, *Portrait of the Artist as a Young Man* (1916), is required reading for all those who take literature seriously. Born in Dublin, Ireland, to a family that struggled financially but maintained a façade of respectability, Joyce left Ireland in 1904, after graduating from the University of Dublin and, after 1920, lived the majority of his life in France. The influences of Dublin, his education, and the Roman Catholic Church, however, are evident throughout all of his writing. *The Dubliners* (1914), *Ulysses* (1922), and *Finnegans Wake* (1939) are among his most famous works.

Lardner, Ring[gold] (1885–1933) Born in Niles, Michigan, Lardner spent his earliest years as a sports reporter for the Chicago *Tribune,* where his experiences resulted in a comical epistolary novel, *You Know Me Al.* Years of magazine writing produced a series of narratives written in deliberately ungrammatical dialect (e.g., "The Golden Honeymoon," 1922), bitterly satirizing the middle class. A friend to and drinking partner with F. Scott Fitzgerald on Long Island from 1923 to 1924, Lardner's scorn of American life resulted in a series of satirical nonsense plays, most of which were collected in *What of It?* (1925) and the posthumous *First and Last* (1934). He wrote *June Moon* (1929) with George S. Kaufman. He died of a heart ailment in 1933.

Lewis, Sinclair (1885–1951) American social satirist Sinclair Lewis was born in Sauk Centre, Minnesota. After attending Yale University, Lewis took jobs in publishing in New York City. He achieved success with his fifth novel, *Main Street* (1920), and solidified his reputation with four succeeding novels: *Babbitt* (1922), his best work, about a self-centered, ignorant real estate agent; *Arrowsmith* (1925), for which was awarded but refused the Pulitzer Prize; *Elmer Gantry* (1927); and *Dodsworth* (1929). After winning the Nobel Prize in 1930, the literary quality of his works declined, although *It Can't Happen Here* (1935) is a prescient portrayal of fascism in America. A noisy, boisterous man, and an alcoholic, Lewis died alone in Rome, Italy.

McKay, Claude (1889–1948) McKay, one of eleven children, was born in Jamaica and raised by an older brother. While studying cabinetry, he was introduced to literature by a British linguist. After publishing two books written in Jamaican dialect, *Songs of Jamaica* and *Constab Ballads* (both 1912), he studied at Booker T. Washington's Tuskegee Institute in Alabama. He moved to Harlem in 1914 and wrote "If We Must Die" in 1917. *Harlem Shadows* appeared in 1922. In that same year he went to Moscow, and he remained in Europe until 1934. His three novels, about the problems of black adjustment in a white society, were written abroad. After returning to America, McKay became a Catholic and worked at the National Catholic Youth Organization in Chicago before his death in 1948.

Mencken, H[enry] L[ouis] (1880–1956) Born in Baltimore, the city with which he would always be associated, Mencken was the son of a cigar manufacturer. He began a journalistic career at the age of nineteen, moving to the paper that is most associated with him, *The Baltimore Sun,* in 1906. A consistent opponent of Puritanism ("the great artists of the world are seldom Puritans and often not even respectable"), his libertarian views on all manner of subjects from art to politics to social Darwinism, offended many and made him a hero to others. He published several books of his collected writings as "Prejudices," wrote a seminal study of the American language (1919 and revised editions in later years), and an account of his career in three volumes: *Happy Days 1880–1892* (1940), *Newspaper Days 1899–1906* (1942), and *Heathen Days 1890–1936* (1943). His epitaph reads, with characteristic irreverence, "If after I depart this vale you ever remember me and have thought to please my ghost, forgive some sinner, and wink your eye at some homely girl."

Moore, Marianne (1887–1972) Moore's early years were spent in Missouri, where she was born, but it was not until she began publishing her poems in the college literary magazine at Bryn Mawr that she came into her own. Publication of poems in *The Egoist, Poetry,* and *Others* followed. She moved to Greenwich Village. Her first book, *Poems,* was assembled from work selected and then published without Moore's knowledge in England by Hilda Doolittle, Moore's acquaintance from Bryn Mawr. After winning a prize for *Observations* (1924) from the Dial Press, she served as editor for the magazine *The Dial.* In 1929 she moved with her mother to Brooklyn, where she stayed, on Cumberland Street, until 1966, when she returned to Greenwich Village. A retiring person of diverse interests— baseball, automobiles, biology—she won the Bollingen Prize, a Pulitzer Prize, and the National Book Award for her collections of verse*: The Pangolin and Other Verse* (1936)*, What Are the Years* (1941)*, Nevertheless* (1944)*, Tell Me, Tell Me* (1966)*,* which were admired by T. S. Eliot, W. H. Auden, and Theodore Roethke.

O'Neill, Eugene (1888–1953) Born in New York City into a family of actors much like the one portrayed in *Long Day's Journey into Night* (1940) (drug addicted mother, alcoholic father), O'Neill spent his early years in New London, Connecticut, and New York. In 1909 he secretly married his twenty-year-old girlfriend. He traveled in Central America, worked at odd jobs, tried to kill himself, drank, had numerous affairs, developed tuberculosis, and started writing plays in Provincetown, Massachusetts, in 1914, and acted in some of them as well. In 1920 he began to write the distinctive expressionist plays that made his name, and he eventually produced *Desire Under the Elms* (1924) and *Strange Interlude* (1927). He stopped drinking but relapsed for brief bursts throughout the rest of his life. In 1936 O'Neill won the Nobel Prize for Literature. He finished *The Iceman Cometh* in 1939, although the play was not produced until 1946, and wrote *Long Day's Journey Into Night* in 1940. After severe illnesses brought on by intemperate living, he moved into a Boston hotel in 1951. He died of a degenerative brain disease in 1953.

Pound, Ezra (1885–1972) Born in Idaho, Ezra Pound moved to Pennsylvania when his father took a job at the mint there. A prodigy, he entered the University of Pennsylvania at fifteen because of his abilities in Latin. After transferring to Hamilton College, from which he graduated in 1905, he studied romance languages and tried teaching in a variety of colleges but was not happy until he moved to London where he made many literary acquaintances, including W. B. Yeats, who introduced him to the work of James Joyce, and managed to assist Robert Frost, T. S. Eliot, and D. H. Lawrence. He became associated with Harriet Monroe and *Poetry* magazine. In 1921 he started to write and publish his cantos, and in 1922 he edited and greatly improved Eliot's *The Waste Land* (1922). *Personae*, Pound's collected poems, was published in 1926. Pound attempted to influence Washington on economic policy on a visit there in 1939. During World War II, Pound broadcast anti-Semitic remarks and was indicted for treason. He was found to be of unsound mind and was placed in St. Elizabeth's Hospital in Washington, D.C. He continued to publish his cantos. Released in 1958, Pound made one final trip to America in 1969 before dying in Italy in 1972.

Rogers, Will (1879–1935) American actor and humorist. Proud of his Cherokee heritage, Will Rogers first was an Indian cowboy riding in cattle drives from Texas to Kansas. He used this experience to perform roping tricks in vaudeville and later the movies. However, it was his dialogue and jokes that made him popular throughout America, and even Europe. By the early twentieth century, Rogers was writing newspaper columns that reached an estimated 40 million readers, and he was one of the first personalities to have regularly scheduled radio broadcasts. His Sunday night show highlighted his humor and philosophical comments about life, government, and economics of the times. In addition, Rogers starred in more than 21 movies as a cowboy. In 1935, he flew with his friend Wiley Post to Alaska, reporting the wonders he saw in a newspaper column for *The New York Times*. Both men were killed in a plane crash that shocked and grieved the world.

Roosevelt, Franklin Delano (1882–1945) Thirty-second president of the United States, serving from 1933–1945. Leading the nation during the Great Depression and World War II, and as the only U.S. president to be elected to third and fourth terms, Roosevelt left a lasting legacy. Entering politics after graduating from Columbia Law School, Roosevelt suffered from polio in 1921 at 39 but went on to be elected governor of New York in 1928 and president of the United States in 1932, when the country had almost 25 percent of its population unemployed. His "New Deal" reforms sought to put people to work with government programs, regulate the banking industry, and establish a social safety net for the elderly, today's social security system. Whereas the majority of Americans accepted Roosevelt's ideas, there was a vocal minority who believed his policies were dangerous to a strong economy. The country's economy, however, was slowly recovering when the war in Europe became America's top priority, following the bombing of Pearl Harbor in Hawaii in 1941. Roosevelt spent the last of his four terms running the war and planning for a peace that he hoped would last longer than the one between World Wars I and II. His famous saying, "The only thing we have to fear is fear itself," is indicative of his positive belief in the American spirit.

Stein, Gertrude (1874–1946) Born into a German Jewish family in Pennsylvania, Stein at age six moved to California but returned east to attend school in Baltimore and then at Radcliffe College, where she studied marine biology and anatomy. Thanks to shrewd managing of resources, Stein was free to travel throughout Europe, which increasingly became home to her, and to buy modern art (paintings by Gaugin, Cézanne, Degas, Toulouse-Lautrec, and her friend Pablo Picasso). She held salons in Paris in 1905 and began writing. In 1907 Stein met her lifelong companion Alice B. Toklas, and after World War I established herself, famously, at 27, rue de Fleurus, where Hemingway, Anderson, Fitzgerald, and a host of European writers, painters, artists, and intellectuals gathered.

Steinbeck, John (1902–1968) American novelist. Born in Salinas, California, Steinbeck's major works depicted life among farm workers in the rural areas of that state. Whereas Steinbeck worked his way through college at Stanford University, he never graduated but instead went to New York to try writing. Unsuccessful at first, he returned to California, publishing his first successful work, *Tortilla Flat,* in 1935, a novel about Hispanic workers living around Monterey. Traveling through the state, he interviewed and wrote about those he met. His novels *In Dubious Battle* (1936)*, Of Mice and Men* (1937)*, The Grapes of Wrath* (1939, for which he won the Pulitzer prize)*,* and *East of Eden* (1952) are examples of his social commentaries. Steinbeck was awarded the Nobel prize for literature in 1962, six years before his death.

Stevens, Wallace (1879–1955) Stevens's childhood was spent in Reading, Pennsylvania, at the Reading Boy's School. Always writing, he attended Harvard and obtained his degree in three years. Stevens tried journalism and wanted to devote himself to writing, but his father insisted that he earn a law degree. He did so and was admitted to the bar in 1904. Stevens married Elsie Moll in 1904. He established himself as an insurance man but continued to publish poems in *Poetry* and other magazines. In 1923 Knopf, on the advice of Carl Van Vechten, brought out *Harmonium.* Family duties precluded more writing until 1936 when *Ideas of Order* appeared, establishing Stevens as a major poet. *The Man with the Blue Guitar* followed. Stevens traveled with Robert Frost in Florida and broke his hand trying to punch out Ernest Hemingway. *Transport to Summer* (1947) and *The Auroras of Autumn* (1950) preceded the magisterial *Collected Poems* of 1954. Yale awarded Stevens an honorary degree in 1952. He died of cancer in 1955.

Terkel, Louis (Studs) (1912–2008) American journalist. After graduating with a law degree from the University of Chicago in 1934, Terkel was part of the Federal Writers' Project in the 1930s, moving on to radio as a news commentator during World War II. He was blacklisted from the entertainment industry in 1953, after being investigated by Senator Joseph McCarthy's House Un-American Activities Committee for his criticism of American businesses' treatment of its workers. Within a few years, however, Terkel was writing for the *Chicago Sunday Times* and began a daily radio program, "The Studs Terkel Show," on which he reported and commented on current events. By the 1970s, he had written five books, some of which included his interviews with those who had endured the Great Depression. *Hard Times* (1970) and *Working* (1974) are accounts of the lives of ordinary working people. For *The Good War* (1985), Terkel won a Pulitzer prize, and in 2008, he completed his last book, *Touch and Go: A Memoir.* He was remembered by those in print, radio, and television as one who never stopped asking questions and who, at the age of 96, said he did not fear death.

Toomer, Jean (1894–1967) Born in Washington D.C., Toomer graduated from Dunbar High School in the District and attended four different colleges. For a time he sold cars, worked in a shipyard, and taught physical education. After visiting New York in 1919 and meeting Waldo Frank, Kenneth Burke, and Hart Crane, Toomer started publishing in *The Dial, Double Dealer, The Crisis,* and other literary magazines. His experimental book *Cane* appeared in 1923. Toomer eventually settled in a Quaker community in Pennsylvania. He published only one other book in his lifetime—*Essentials* (1931)—although after his death and the resurgence of interest in *Cane, The Collected Poems of Jean Toomer* appeared.

Van Vechten, Carl (1880–1964) Van Vechten was born into a well-off family in Cedar Rapids, Iowa, and graduated from the University of Chicago. He moved to New York from the Midwest and became music and arts critic for *The New York Times.* He then began writing fiction, beginning with the satirical *Peter Whiffle* (1922), but it was not until his empathetic picture of life in Harlem, *Nigger Heaven,* appeared in 1926 that he achieved a solid artistic success. Always sympathetic to black culture and to alternative life styles, he stopped writing in 1932 and devoted the rest of his life to photography. His portraits of American artists and writers, especially African Americans, document the cultural life of the first half of the twentieth century.

Williams, William Carlos (1883–1963) American physician and writer. Born in New Jersey, Williams put the American idiom to imaginative use in his writing and used experiences from everyday life as the focus of his poetry. He graduated from University of Pennsylvania Medical School and interned both in New York City and Europe. For 50 years, Williams delivered babies as a pediatrician in his home state. While practicing medicine, Williams was also a prolific poet whose poems were considered part of the modernist movement; he counted among his friends the poets Hilda Doolittle, T.S. Eliot, and Ezra Pound. He is credited with helping many young writers, especially in the years after his retirement from medicine. He also wrote short stories, plays, and several novels.

Wright, Richard (1908–1960) American novelist. Born in Mississippi, Wright was the son of a sharecropper and a school teacher, Ella Wilson, whose life strongly influenced her son. Wright remembers his early years as marked by poverty and struggle. His mother, abandoned by his father, moved back to live with her parents, and when Wright's maternal grandparents were unyielding in their strict adherence to their religious beliefs, Wright found himself caught between his responsibility to his mother, who was ill, and his fervent curiosity and questions about prejudice against blacks in the South. With only an eighth grade education, Wright taught himself to read the classics and eventually moved to Chicago where he became a postal worker, was a member of the Federal Writers' Project in the 1930s, and began writing his autobiography, which was eventually published as *Black Boy* in 1945. Although a bestseller, *Black Boy* was condemned by some in the South. His novel *Native Son* (1940) had been published earlier to positive reviews. He ultimately moved to New York City where he was part of the literary movement known as the Harlem Renaissance. After World War II, the anti-Communist furor present in the United States persuaded him to move to France in 1946, even though he had only attended some early Communist Party meetings. He obtained French citizenship and continued to write, mainly essays, articles, and speeches. In 1991, the Library of America published Wright's complete autobiography including depictions of the tumultuous years in Chicago and New York.

Further Reading

Chapter 1. American Modernism

Kazin, Alfred. *On Native Grounds: An Interpretation of Modern American Prose Literature.* New York: Harcourt, rpt. 1995.

Kenner, Hugh. *A Homemade World: The American Modernist Writers.* Baltimore: Johns Hopkins University Press, rpt. 1989.

Miller, J. Hillis. *Poets of Reality: Six Twentieth-Century Writers.* New York: Belknap Press, 1965.

North, Michael. *The Dialectic of Modernism: Race, Language and Twentieth-Century Literature.* New York: Oxford University Press, 1994.

Taubman, Howard. *The Making of the American Theater.* New York: Putnam, 1967.

Chapter 2. The Politics and Culture of Modernism

Carroll, Joseph. *Evolution and Literary Theory.* Columbia: University of Missouri Press, 1995.

Eliot, T. S. *Selected Essays.* London: Faber, 1954.

Kenner, Hugh. *The Pound Era.* Berkeley: University of California Press, 1973.

Matthiessen, F. O. *The Achievement of T. S. Eliot.* Oxford: Oxford University Press, 1958.

Nadel, Ira B., ed. *The Cambridge Companion to Ezra Pound* (Cambridge Companions to Literature). New York: Cambridge University Press, 1999.

Stanford, Donald E. *Revolution and Convention in Modern Poetry: Studies in Ezra Pound, T.S. Eliot, Wallace Stevens, Edwin Arlington Robinson, and Yvor Winters.* Newark: University of Delaware Press, 1983.

Chapter 3. The Lost Generation

Baker, Carlos. *Hemingway: The Writer as Artist.* Princeton: Princeton University Press, 1972.

Bruccoli, Matthew J. *Some Sort of Epic Grandeur.* New York: Harcourt, 1998.

DeFazio, Albert J. *The Sun Also Rises.* Farmington, Michigan: Gale, 2000.

Kazin, Alfred. *On Native Grounds.* New York: Reynal and Hitchcock, 1942.

Kuehl, John. *F. Scott Fitzgerald: A Study of the Short Fiction.* Boston: Twayne, 1991.

Lathbury, Roger. *The Great Gatsby.* Farmington, Michigan: Gale, 2000.

Young, Philip. *Ernest Hemingway: A Reconsideration.* New York: Harcourt Brace, 1966.

Chapter 4. Modernist American Fiction

Davis, Robert G. *John Dos Passos.* Minneapolis: University of Minnesota Press, 1962.

Hlavsa, Virginia V. James. *Faulkner and the Thoroughly Modern Novel.* Charlottesville: University of Virginia Press, 1991.

Hoffman, Daniel. *Faulkner's Country Matters.* Baton Rouge: Louisiana State University Press, 1989.

Moreland, Richard. *Faulkner and Modernism.* Madison: University of Wisconsin Press, 1990.

"Selected Resources on William Faulkner," <http://www.unf.edu/library/guides/faulkner.html>

Wagner-Martin, Linda. *Dos Passos: Artist as American.* Austin: University of Texas Press, 1979.

Chapter 5. The Harlem Renaissance

Baker, Houston A. *Modernism and the Harlem Renaissance.* Chicago: University of Chicago Press, 1987.

Powell, Richard J., et. al. *Rhapsodies in Black.* Berkeley: University of California Press, 1997.

Singh, Amritjit. et. al., eds. *The Harlem Renaissance: Revaluations.* New York: Garland, 1989.

Wintz, Cary D. *The Politics and Aesthetics of the "New Negro" Literature.* New York: Garland, 1996.

Chapter 6. Modernism in Poetry and Drama

Brietzke, Zander. *The Aesthetics of Failure: Dynamic Structure in the Plays of Eugene O'Neill.* Jefferson, N.C.: McFarland, 2001.

Bloom, Harold. *Wallace Stevens: The Poems of Our Climate.* Ithaca, N.Y.: Cornell University Press, 1977.

Floyd, Virginia, ed. *Eugene O'Neill, A World View.* New York: Ungar, 1979.

Gelb, Arthur and Barbara. *O'Neill.* New York: Peter B. Smith, 1988.

Hoffman, Tyler. *Robert Frost and the Politics of Poetry.* Hanover, N.H.: Middlebury College Press, 2001.

Mariani, Paul L. *William Carlos Williams: A New World Naked.* New York: Norton, 1990.

"Theater Websites" <http://www.lib.washington.edu/subject/Drama/elweb.html>

Chapter 7. The Great Depression (1929–1939)—The Years That Defined an Era

Casey, Janet Galligani, ed. *The Novel and the American Left: Critical Essays on Depression-Era Fiction.* Iowa City: University of Iowa Press, 2004.

Egan, Timothy. *The Worst Hard Times: The Untold Story of Those who Survived the Great American Dust Bowl.* New York: Houghton Mifflin Company, 2005.

Fischer, Kim. "Great Depression, great creativity." <http://www.temple.edu/newsroom/2008_2009/12/stories/depression_creativity.htm?pv=Y>

Mangione, Jerre. *The Dream and the Deal: the FWP 1935-1939.* Boston: Little Brown,1972.

McElvaine, Robert. *The Great Depression*. New York: Times Books, Random House, 1984. <http://www.woodyguthrie.org> accessed May 4,2009

Taylor, David. *The Soul of a People: The WPA Writers Project Uncovers Depression America.* Hoboken: John Wiley & Sons, 2009.

Index